FAILURES OF
THE LEGAL
IMAGINATION

ALAN WATSON

FAILURES OF

THE LEGAL

IMAGINATION

upp

PHILADELPHIA

UNIVERSITY OF PENNSYLVANIA PRESS

Library of Congress Cataloging-in-Publication Data

Watson, Alan.
  Failures of the legal imagination.
  Includes index.
  1. Law—Interpretation and construction—History.
I. Title.
K290.W38   1988   340'.09   87-35806
ISBN 0-8122-8089-X

Designed by Adrianne Onderdonk Dudden

for James Walker Watson

and his grandchildren,
David, Ann, and Sarah

CONTENTS

Abbreviations ix
Preface xiii
Acknowledgments xv

ONE
*The Law of Delict and Quasi-Delict
in the French* Code Civil
1

TWO
Legal Evolution and Legislation
35

THREE
Medical Malpractice Law in Ancient Rome
65

FOUR
Opportunism and Pragmatism in the Law
87

FIVE
Natural Law and English Legal Positivism
107

SIX
Some Legal Phenomena
133

Index
157

ABBREVIATIONS

Baker, *Introduction*

J. H. Baker, *Introduction to English Legal History*, 2nd ed. (London: Butterworths, 1979)

BGB

Bürgerliches Gesetzbuch

C.

Codex Justiniani

C. Th.

Codex Theodosianus

Coing, *Handbuch*

H. Coing, *Handbuch der Quellen und Literatur der neueren europäischen Rechtsgeschichte*, 1– (Munich; Beck, 1973–   )

Coing, *Privatrecht*, 1

H. Coing, *Europäisches Privatrecht, 1500 bis 1800*, 1 (Munich: Beck, 1985)

D.

Digestum Justiniani

Fenet, *Travaux préparatoires*

P. A. Fenet, *Recueil complet des travaux préparatoires du Code Civil*, 1–15 (Paris: Ducessois, 1827)

G.

Gai Institutiones

h.t.	The same title of Justinian's *Digest* or *Code* as in the preceding text.
J.	*Institutiones Justiniani*
Kaser, *Privatrecht*, 1, 2	M. Kaser, *Das römische Privatrecht*, 1, 2, 2nd ed. (Munich: Beck, 1971, 1975)
Lenel, *Edictum*	O. Lenel, *Das Edictum Perpetuum*, 3rd ed. (Leipzig: Tauchnitz, 1927)
Locré, *Législation*	J. G. de Locré, *La Législation civile, commerciale, et criminelle de la France*, 1–31 (Paris, 1827–32)
Milsom, *Foundations*	S. F. C. Milsom, *Historical Foundations of the Common Law*, 2nd ed. (Toronto: Butterworths, 1981)
Pollock and Maitland, *History*, 1, 2	F. Pollock and F. W. Maitland, *The History of English Law*, 2nd ed., reissued with an introduction by S. F. C. Milsom (Cambridge: Cambridge University Press, 1968)
pr.	*principium* (the first, unnumbered, part of a text in some Roman legal sources, including Justinian's *Digest*)
Rotondi, *Leges*	G. Rotondi, *Leges publicae populi romani* (Milan: Società editrice libreria, 1912)
Watson, *Civil Law*	A. Watson, *The Making of the Civil Law* (Cambridge, Mass.: Harvard University Press, 1981)
Watson, *Evolution*	A. Watson, *The Evolution of Law* (Baltimore: Johns Hopkins University Press, 1985)

Watson, *Law Making*

A. Watson, *Law Making in the Later Roman Republic* (Oxford: Clarendon Press, 1974)

Watson, "Legal Change"

A. Watson, "Legal Change: Sources of Law and Legal Culture," *University of Pennsylvania Law Review* 131 (1983): 1121–1157

Watson, *Obligations*

A. Watson, *The Law of Obligations in the Later Roman Republic* (Oxford: Clarendon Press, 1965)

Watson, *Persons*

A. Watson, *The Law of Persons in the Later Roman Republic* (Oxford: Clarendon Press, 1967)

Watson, *Property*

A. Watson, *The Law of Property in the Later Roman Republic* (Oxford: Clarendon Press, 1968)

Watson, *Sources of Law*

A. Watson, *Sources of Law, Legal Change, and Ambiguity* (Philadelphia: University of Pennsylvania Press, 1984)

Watson, *Transplants*

A. Watson, *Legal Transplants, An Approach to Comparative Law* (Charlottesville: University Press of Virginia, 1974)

Watson, *XII Tables*

A. Watson, *Rome of the XII Tables, Persons and Property* (Princeton, N.J.: Princeton University Press, 1975)

ZSS

Zeitschrift der Savigny Stiftung (romanistische Abteilung)

PREFACE

This book grew out of the Julius Rosenthal lectures that I had the honor and delight of giving at the Northwestern School of Law in October 1987. Chapters 1, 3, and 5 are versions of the three lectures, and each is devoted to a striking example of "failures of the legal imagination," the title of the lecture series. Quite deliberately, each lecture deals with a very different theme. In Chapter 1, I want to show that even when legislators are dedicated to making a new start, they are often so blinkered by the legal tradition that, with regard to important branches of the law, they put forward no coherent social, political, or economic message. A major subtheme is that, contrary to the accepted view, the extent of the Reception of Roman law in civil law systems cannot be limited to or measured by the acceptance of Roman legal solutions. Chapter 3, the second lecture, is devoted to the proposition that even when it is the "setting in life" that determines the scope of legal rules in a particular society, the rules may still reflect their origins hundreds of years later in very changed circumstances. My aim in the third lecture, Chapter 5, is to demonstrate that important legal scholars and theorists, too, do not easily escape the parameters of legal debate fixed centuries before.

But the lectures, when written and assembled side by side,

opened up new vistas. Chapter 2 takes up the theme of Chapter 1 and links with aspects of Chapter 3 to show more generally that legislation—which can be the most radical way of developing law—often fails to live up to anything like its potential to provide a society with law geared toward precise political and social goals. Indeed, though law is politics, governments often have little interest in making much law or in having a particular political, social, or economic message in their laws. Chapter 4 deals with a consequence of this failure to provide adequate statutory law for the society: opportunism on the part of jurists and judges to develop the law.

Instead of drawing conclusions, I hope to show in Chapter 6 that the arguments in the book make fully comprehensible some otherwise very puzzling phenomena, such as the enormous role that the Roman state allowed jurists—individuals with no official position—to play in developing private law, and the remarkable lack of interest that societies display in communicating law to those affected by it. Finally, I attempt to apply the lessons of the book to provide a key to one of the fundamental problems of legal history, the development of English common law.

Many of the sources used for this book are not readily accessible, so I have made considerable use of quotations. In all cases the translations are my own.

ACKNOWLEDGMENTS

A special debt of thanks is owed to the faculty, staff, and students of the Northwestern University School of Law for the outstanding grace and generosity of their welcome to my wife and me when I delivered the Julius Rosenthal lectures on 26, 27, and 28 October 1987. No one, perhaps, should be singled out, but I cannot forbear to mention Professor Ian R. MacNeil and his wife, Nancy, who offered us the warmth of their home, Dean Robert W. Bennett, and his assistant Robin Accola.

Gratitude, equally heartfelt, is also owed to friends who read and criticized various drafts of this book. John W. Cairns, above all, read and commented in detail on at least one version of every chapter, as did Michael H. Hoeflich. Stephen B. Burbank did the same for Chapters 1, 2, and 5. I was offered expert guidance on Chapter 1 by Bernard Rudden and on Chapter 5 by Martin Krygier and Neil MacCormick. Other friends, too numerous to mention, discussed many points with me. To all I am grateful.

Alan Watson
Philadelphia
1 November 1987

CHAPTER ONE

THE LAW OF DELICT AND QUASI-DELICT IN THE FRENCH *CODE CIVIL*

From the eleventh century until the successful modern codification movement in the eighteenth century, European law in the West presents a picture of overwhelming complexity. There were many strands to the law: local custom, feudal law, local legislation, canon law, and Roman law. The same individual in different aspects of his or her life might be subject to various courts: the feudal court of one's lord, the canon law court of the church, the court of the village or town, with possibly an appeal to a court of different outlook such as the Parlement de Paris or the Reichskammergericht. Two systems of law, Roman law and canon law, were regarded as having transnational significance, even though the extent to which Roman law was received in practice varied from territory to territory. Roman law and canon law worked upon each other, with Roman law the dominant partner, to form eventually the *ius commune*, virtually a common learned law for Western Europe. In any state, of course, the impact of the *ius commune* depended on the strength of the other local elements.[1]

The importance of customary law in the mixture is easily underrated, for various reasons. There was a profusion of customary legal systems, varying greatly from one another and often having very limited territorial jurisdiction. Customary law was not studied in the universities of medieval or Renaissance Europe. It lacks the charm of sophistication of Roman law or of the *ius commune*. Above all, with the rise of the modern world, much of customary law was abandoned, or if it did survive, it was in a very different guise. An inhabitant of today's world, whether from a civil law or a common law country, will feel more at ease reading the *Institutes* of Justinian than the *Coutumes de Normandie*.[2]

Nonetheless, during the eleventh to eighteenth centuries, the two primary intersecting strands in Western legal development were local customary law and Roman law (often in the form of the *ius commune*), with the latter, gradually or more swiftly, acting to fill gaps in, modify, render more sophisticated, or replace the former.[3] The modern civil codes are largely the result of this intertwining. But the specific contribution of each strand is not easily determined. Thus, to estimate the force of the Roman law strand, one must find the answer to a question that I have never seen raised. What was the impact of Roman rules on the legal rules in modern civil codes when the Roman rules were inappropriate either because of changed societal conditions or attitudes or because for some reason the Roman rules themselves were underdeveloped? If the Roman rules were not accepted, must one simply deny any input and restrict the Reception of Roman law to instances of direct borrowing? Is nonacceptance rejection? This certainly seems to have been the attitude of some distinguished scholars who have, perhaps, not quite seen the issue. Thus, Jean Brissaud regards codification in France as a victory for customary law over Roman law.[4] For Paul Viollet, "Our codes, considered from the historical point of view, are the concentration and unification of the old French law, dispersed, and often divergent, in the royal *ordonnances* and the customs."[5] And Rudolf B. Schlesinger bluntly states:

On one point, however, there can be no reasonable difference of opinion: The old adage, all-too-frequently repeated, that the civilian codes presently in force are merely a modernized version of Roman law, is simply nonsense. In many respects, the solutions adopted by the codifiers were not traditional; and of the traditional ones, many were not Roman. The late Professor Reginald Parker was probably right when he said: "I seriously believe it would not be difficult to establish, if such a thing could be statistically approached, that the majority of legal institutes, even within the confines of private law, of a given civil law country are not necessarily of Roman origin.[6]

The implication seems to be that if Roman solutions were not adopted, Roman law had no impact. A further implication seems to be that the impact of Roman law was not as great as has been supposed and hence for an understanding of the modern law may be safely ignored.

The matter, I believe, is not so simple. I intend no paradox, but this first chapter will be devoted to an investigation of the Reception of Roman law when the Roman rules were not received. The issue is, what happens to the law upon codification when the Roman legal rules are obviously inappropriate and hence not accepted? Each situation of fact and law will be different, and I do not intend to build up a general theory. By temperament and training, I can only proceed from detailed analysis and I wish here to concentrate on the articles that appear in the French *code civil* of 1804 under the heading "Delicts and Quasi-Delicts":

1382. Every action of a human which causes injury to another binds the person through whose fault it occurred to make it good.

1383. Everyone is responsible for the injury which he caused not only by his action, but also by his negligence or imprudence.

1384. One is responsible not only for the injury which one causes by one's own action, but also for that which is caused by the action of persons for whom one is responsible, or of things which one has under one's guard.

The father, and the mother after the death of the husband, are responsible for the injury caused by their minor children living with them;

Masters and employers for the injury caused by their servants and agents in the functions for which they employed them;

Teachers and craftsmen for the injury caused by their pupils and apprentices during the time that they were under their surveillance.

The above responsibility lies, unless the father and the mother, teachers and craftsmen prove that they could not have prevented the action which gives rise to the responsibility.

1385. The owner of an animal or the person who makes use of it, while it is subject to his use, is responsible for the injury which the animal has caused, whether the animal was under his guard, whether it had wandered off or escaped.

1386.   The owner of a building is responsible for the injury caused by its fall when that occurred as a consequence of a defect in maintenance or by a fault in its construction.[7]

To begin with, we will take these articles at face value on the subject of the basis of liability. The relationship among the five provisions is by no means clear. Articles 1382 and 1383, dealing with responsibility for one's own actions, make liability clearly dependent on fault, including negligence; and, though this is not expressly said, the normal burden of proving negligence will lie with the plaintiff. But how can one understand the basis of liability in art. 1384 for the behavior of persons for whom one is responsible or for things under one's guard? With one crucial exception, nothing is said about the basis of liability. The first issue to which no answer is given directly is whether the person for whom one is responsible must have been at fault for liability to accrue. One might at first say no, since minor children will often be under the age at which any fault could be attributed to them. Nothing is said to divide minor children into categories, and it is a principle of French law that one cannot make a distinction where the law makes none.[8] Nevertheless, in favor of a positive response is the fact that a master is liable for injuries caused by the action of a servant. Is a master liable for his own behavior only if he is at fault, but is to be automatically and strictly liable for the injury caused by a servant who was without fault? Common sense would suggest not. Thus, this article does not yield a clear answer, negative or positive. Nor is there any indication on the face of the article whether for liability to be caused by a thing, the thing must have been defective.

When we look elsewhere for the basis of liability, in the behavior of the "superior," we are left in just as great a state of confusion. For injury caused by the behavior of servants and agents and things, there is no clear indication whether for liability the "superior" himself had to have been at fault. One might feel that the "superior" here was always absolutely liable, even if free from fault, since the sole exception to liability—applying expressly to parents, teachers, and craftsmen—is not stated so as to apply to the master of servants and agents or the guardians of things. But it might be rash to draw such a conclusion. And does art. 1384 really equate the liability of the "superior" for the behavior of persons with his liability for the behavior of things? We should suppose so, since they are treated without distinction in the same article. But that conclusion seems unpalatable. The exception, too, causes problems. Parents, teachers, and craftsmen are excused from liability for injury caused by their children, pupils, and apprentices only if they can show that they could not have prevented the action. The basis of liability here is not that for one's own actions in arts. 1382 and 1383; at the very least, the burden of proof here has been shifted to the defendant.

More than that, it seems that the defendant is not free from liability if he proves he was not negligent; he must show that he could not have prevented the behavior. And we must remember that we cannot tell whether the behavior in question had to be negligent or worse on the part of the actual doer. Art. 1385 in its turn does not on its face provide us with an answer to the two relevant questions: whether the animal had to be at "fault" for liability to be imposed on the master or operator, or whether for liability the master had to be at fault in allowing the animal to cause injury. Art. 1386 is clearer in its meaning but leaves us no less confused. The owner of a building that collapses and causes injury is liable for the damage in either of two cases: where the collapse was the result of poor maintenance (fault on the part of the owner) and where the collapse was the result of a fault in the construction (a defect in the building). But this second case leaves us with several problems to which the articles, on their face, provide no solution. First, why is the owner liable even when he is without fault—he may have had no part in the construction and may have been unable to check for defects in construction—when for his own behavior he is liable only when at fault? Second, why is a distinction made with regard to a building in art. 1386 and things under one's guard in art. 1384—and what is the nature of that distinction? Third, why does art. 1386 speak expressly only of buildings and not of immovables in general? For example, a tree may fall if it has not been properly looked after or if it is defective. In enumerating the problems of the basis of liability under the five articles we should finally note that the heading refers to both delicts and quasi-delicts, but neither term appears in the text of the articles.[9] The terminology is not further elucidated, nor is any difference in the basis of liability for one or the other.

We are still not yet concerned with the intention of the drafters of the code. But in light of what has just been said, it should be admitted with regard to the basis of liability both that the articles were poorly drafted and that the drafters either were hopelessly confused or had no consistent policy. What explanation can be found for these facts? It should be emphasized here that the issue is not just of theoretical significance. The basis of liability under these five articles is one of the most controversial issues in the interpretation of the *code civil* as the merest glance at the battery of apparatus, from both "doctrine" and "jurisprudence," laid out in the *Petit Code Dalloz* edition, would show.

In response to the confusion, two answers must be given: the short and the long one. The short answer offers a basic explanation. The long answer then demonstrates the accuracy of the short answer and adds detail.

First, the short answer. The confusion occurs above all in situations in which Roman solutions, as set out in Justinian's *Corpus Juris Civilis*, were inappropriate and could not be expressly used because of changed social conditions and societal attitudes—but in which those solutions or texts had a hidden impact.

Thus, in arts. 1382 and 1383, the basis of liability for one's own behavior—of which rather more must be said later—is obviously based on fault. This was the position in Roman law, especially under the *lex Aquilia*.[10] But the first problem that concerns us arises only in art. 1384, which covers liability for the actions of persons for whom one was responsible. Under Roman law, the dependent person for whom a superior was responsible would be a son in the power of his father (a *filiusfamilias*) or a slave. A slave had no legal standing in private law and could not be sued directly, and a *filiusfamilias* owned no property and was not worth suing. The head of the family, the *paterfamilias*, was logically the only person who could be sued, and liability vested in him—as did, for example, rights regarding the contracts of sons or slaves—because he was the head of the family. Roman law gave the victim an action against the owner or father as the *paterfamilias* for the wrongful behavior, whether malicious or negligent, of a slave or son, but the defendant could avoid condemnation in the money sum by handing over the slave or son to the victim in noxal surrender before judgment was pronounced.[11] The notion was therefore a primitive form of limited liability. The wrongful behavior of a dependent could result in a loss of his or her "superior" but only up to the worth of the wrongdoer. Fault on the part of the "superior" was irrelevant—because liability was based solely on his position as head of the family—except that it might in some circumstances exclude his right to hand over the actual perpetrator in noxal surrender.[12] Fault on the part of the dependent was necessary, just as fault alone made a person of independent status (*sui juris*) liable for injury caused by his or her behavior. The absence in France of noxal surrender (and of anything equivalent to the Roman *patria potestas*) meant that this neat and satisfactory solution could not be adopted. This resulted—as will be shown in the long answer—in some confusion of thought both among the drafters of the *code civil* and among the French legal scholars who preceded them. Hence the failure in the *code civil* to make liability depend clearly either on fault on the part of the dependent perpetrator or on fault on the part of his or her "superior."

Similarly, there was no obvious, appropriate solution to be found by the drafters of the *code* in Roman law regarding liability for damage caused by things under one's guard. There was no general overriding principle in Roman law concerning liability for damage caused by an inanimate thing—nor was one much needed before the days of steam boilers, the internal combustion engine, and high explosives—but liability for movables occurred in two situations, both of which were classed by the Romans as quasi-delicts. In one, an action was given against a householder from whose dwelling something was thrown or poured onto a way that was commonly used, resulting in damage.[13] The action lay against the householder—simply because he was the householder—whether he did or did not do the throwing, knew of it, or could have prevented it.[14] Ownership of the thing thrown or poured was irrelevant;[15] the action was given in effect against the person who had the thing under his guard. And, of course, there can be no question regarding the injury resulting from a defect in the thing. The Roman approach is sensible, especially in view of the difficulty of proof and because the occupier on any approach would be liable not only for his own behavior but also for that of his sons or slaves; if the occupier had not thrown or poured out the thing, they might have done so.

In the other situation, an action was given against the occupier of a building from or on whose eave or projecting roof something was suspended or placed, above a way commonly used, and whose fall could cause damage.[16] The action did not lie specifically against the person who placed the thing in its dangerous position, and, since no injury had yet occurred, there could be no relevance in the condition of the thing.[17] The approach is reasonable as a preventive device. These are both special cases. If one generalized from them—which obviously one ought not to—then one would come up with the proposition that a person was liable for things under his guard whether or not his own behavior was wrongful, and irrespective of any defect in the thing. This is the way art. 1384 of the *code civil* seems to have been framed, but if this were the intention of the drafters it would be highly inappropriate, for the following reasons. First, it conflicts with the basis of liability for one's own acts, under arts. 1382 and 1383; second, it probably conflicts with art. 1384 regarding the acts of persons for whom one was responsible; and third, it conflicts with art. 1386 concerning the collapse of a building. But Roman law provided no general solution that could be borrowed regarding liability for damage caused by a thing. (As an aside, I wish to interject that it would be truly amazing, would it not, if the formulation here in the *code civil* resulted from the Roman *actio de effusis vel deiectis* ["action for pouring out or throwing down"] and *actio de positis ac suspensis* ["action for placing or suspending"]? Yet that is what I want to show!)

Under Roman law, when an animal caused damage and could be said to be at "fault," a remedy under the *actio de pauperie* lay to the victim against the owner of the animal for the amount of the harm done—but, again, the owner could escape further liability if he chose to surrender the animal.[18] The device of an owner's limited liability was again used. Given that fact, and the fact that the victim had, indeed, suffered loss, it is perfectly understandable that for the *actio de pauperie* to be available the negligence or otherwise of the owner in keeping the animal from causing harm was not an issue. But noxal surrender did not exist in France, so the total acceptance of the solution of the *actio de pauperie* was not obviously appropriate. Yet art. 1385 on its face says nothing about whether the owner or user of an animal is liable without fault for any damage it causes or whether, as in the case of the owner's or user's own behavior, he is liable only if he is at fault. Either interpretation is possible. (It should be remembered that at this stage we are concerned not with the intention of the drafters but rather with their formulation in the *code*.) It will, I hope, be admitted that a pattern in the drafting is emerging. The solution—noxal surrender—of the Roman *actio de pauperie,* in which the owner's negligence in preventing the animal from causing harm was irrelevant, was not acceptable in nineteenth-century France. But since the Romans did not discuss this issue of the owner's negligence regarding the *actio de pauperie,* then neither did art. 1385 clearly set out the basis of the owner's or user's liability.

Two other remedies were available in Roman law for damage caused by animals, and both are relevant here. The *actio de pastu* gave an action when animals fed on the acorns on another's land. This action is not prominent in the Roman sources, the texts are relatively uninformative, and one of two views may be held. On one view (which I favor), the action was available only when a person actually sent his animals to feed on another's land.[19] On another view, which has textual support in the postclassical *Pauli Sententiae,* the action allowed noxal surrender,[20] in which case fault on the part of the owner would be irrelevant. The second action was given under the Edict of the *curule aediles* against someone who had kept a fierce animal (presumably often for gladiatorial games) in such a way that it caused damage where people commonly walked. The basis of liability was exposing people to damage, and no other fault was necessary. Hence the action was penal: a fixed sum was payable if a free human being was killed; the judge decided what was fair if a free human being was injured; and in other cases the penalty was double the loss inflicted.[21] Thus, there were three Roman actions, though the action that was prominent in the Roman sources was the *actio de pauperie.*

The existence of a pattern is confirmed when we look at art. 1386. The "setting in life" of the provision, as a glance at Domat[22] and the discussion of the draft code reveals[23]—and as we shall see in the "long answer"—is in the Roman remedies for *damnum infectum,* that is to say, loss that is threatened but has not yet occurred. In general, as has been mentioned, Roman law gave no remedy for damage caused by a thing, and this was so even for the collapse of a building.[24] But if a neighbor felt threatened by defective elements on another's land, he might approach the praetor, who would command the latter to give security for restitution if the damage occurred—the so-called *cautio damni infecti*. The *cautio* was given on account of threatened injury, which means there must have been a defect in the thing. Hence, even if the injury for which the *cautio* was taken occurred but the defect was not the cause of the injury—for instance, when a storm was so strong that even a sound building might lose its tiles—the owner of the defective property was not liable under the *cautio*.[25] If the owner of the dangerous property failed to give the *cautio*, the praetor would grant the threatened neighbor *missio in possessionem*, or detention of the property.[26]

Because French law did not adopt either *cautio damni infecti* or *missio in possessionem*, there was no remedy for future, threatened damage. Nonetheless, the Roman treatment of *damnum infectum* was the focus for subsequent French discussion of damage by immovable property—there was no other possible part of Roman law to which discussion could be attached since, in the absence of the *cautio*, there was no general remedy for damage caused by an inanimate thing.[27] It is this setting that enables us to provide answers to the three problems set out earlier in connection with art. 1386. First, the owner in France might be liable without fault on his part, because liability in Roman law was based on a defect in the property (which might cause damage). For the Romans, of course, since the defect was observable and the injury foreseeable and made known to the owner, the owner would be at fault if he had failed to carry out the necessary repairs. Second, art. 1386 deals only with immovables because threatened damage by immovable property alone was covered by the Roman remedies. The third problem—why art. 1386 speaks expressly of buildings and not also of trees—requires greater elucidation. The Roman *cautio de damno infecto* was available not only for damage threatened by defective buildings and other human works but also for threatened damage from defective trees.[28] But whereas the praetor provided model formulae in his Edict for threatened damage from human works, he appears not to have given one for damage resulting from trees. Likewise, the jurists did not discuss threatened damage by trees and other natural objects on land in their own right, but only in passing in connection with human works.[29] Most important perhaps, *missio in possessionem* was never discussed in connection with damage threatened from natural objects but only regarding human works, and especially buildings. Subsequent French discussion, therefore, came to speak only of damage by human works, above all by buildings. If the argument up to this point is correct—and detailed evidence will be provided in the long answer—then we have a particular twist in legal development in art. 1386. The basis of liability in art. 1386 was determined by Roman remedies that were not accepted in France, yet because of the emphasis in the Roman sources the French provision appeared to be restricted to damage caused by human immovable works and not also (as in Roman law) to damage from trees.[30]

At this stage, some preliminary conclusions may be drawn, if only to show where the argument is going. In the field of wrongful damage, although Roman law provided a coherent set of remedies, some of those remedies were inappropriate for the France of a later era, partly because of changed social conditions and partly because certain Roman legal notions, such as surrender of dependent persons and animals or the concept of threatened damage, were rejected. Still, the discussion in France that formed the basis of the articles of the *code civil* proceeded on the basis of Roman law, resulting in the appalling confusion apparent in the articles—whether the confusion was mainly in the drafting or also in the minds of the codifiers. It is the corollary to these conclusions that is most important. When Roman law was inappropriate, and even when it was rejected, the drafters were not necessarily freed from its dominance. They did not always find solutions in local custom. They did not always proffer their own coherent solutions.

Now the long answer. To keep it brief, I will deal expressly and at length with only four issues: liability for a thing under one's guard under art. 1384; liability regarding persons for whom one was responsible; liability for an animal under art. 1385; and liability for the fall of a building under art. 1386.

We may find a satisfactory starting point in Jean Domat's *Les Lois Civiles dans Leur Ordre Naturel* (which first appeared between

1689 and 1697). Domat's grand plan was to set out a scheme of Christian law for France in an easily comprehensible arrangement. Four kinds of law, he said, ruled in France.[31] First, the royal ordinances had universal authority over all of France. Second, customs had particular authority in the place where they were observed. Third, Roman law had two uses, first as custom in some places in several matters, second over all of France and on all matters, "consisting in this that one observes everywhere these rules of justice and equity that are called 'written reason,' because they are written in Roman law. Thus, for this second use, Roman law has the same authority as have justice and equity on our reason." Fourth, canon law also contained many rules accepted in France, though some had been rejected. Domat went on to claim that he drew up the plan of the book and the choice of subject matter because the natural law of equity lay in the Roman law and because the study of Roman law was so difficult.[32]

He introduced the discussion of wrongful damage in book 2, title 8:

> One can distinguish three sorts of wrongs from which some damage may arise: those wrongs which amount to a crime or an offense; those wrongs of persons who fail in their agreed on obligations such as a seller who does not deliver the thing sold, a tenant who does not make the repairs he is bound to do; and those wrongs which have no relation with agreements and which do not amount to a crime or an offense, as if light-mindedly one throws something out of a window which spoils a suit; if animals not properly guarded do some damage; if one carelessly causes a fire, if a building which threatens to collapse, not being repaired, falls on another and there causes damage.
>
> Of these three types of wrong, only those of the last category are the subject of this title; because crimes and offenses ought not to be mixed with civil matters, and everything which concerns agreements has been explained in the first book.[33]

The scene is set for the discussion of the topics that interest us, damage caused by things, animals, and buildings. The discussion under this one category seems very lopsided. The headings of the title are: 1. On what is thrown from a house, or can fall from one and cause loss; 2. Of loss caused by animals; 3. Of the loss which may result from the collapse of a building or some new work; 4. Of other kinds of damage caused by fault, without a crime or offense. Pothier, in his *Traité des obligations,* gives very short shrift to *délits* and *quasi-délits,* dismissing the subject in half a section.[34] This approach, which was not restricted to these two lawyers, indicates a disregard for the subject, which was to have enormous consequences and which must be explained. Domat was discussing other kinds of loss caused by fault, "sans crime ni délit." The translation of the word *délit* is by no means immediately obvious. It is not clear whether it is the Roman *delictum* or the *délit* of later French law. Whatever it is, like "crime" it should not, in the eyes of Domat, be mixed with civil matters. The basic idea can be discovered in a roundabout way by looking at what Domat in fact does not treat— since he is concerned with civil law—and examining how other writers, even at a later date, approached the issue.

Domat did not deal with the wrongs that the Romans, as in Justinian's *Institutes,* classed as *delicta,* presumably because, as other writers make plain, they partook of crime. Thus, to take a few examples from other jurisdictions, Sir George Mackenzie, in his *Institutions of the Law of Scotland* (first edition, 1684), did not deal with delicts, but in the final title of the book, "Of Crimes" (4.4), he wrote: "*Private crimes,* called also *delicta,* in the *Civil Law,* oblige the Committers to repair the Dammage, and Interest of the private Party." But he says no more about private crimes. And Marino Guarano in his *Praelectiones ad Institutiones Justiniani in Usum Regni Neapolitani* (1779) claimed (4.1.3): "Vitiositas actus in veris delictis est dolus, in quasi delictis est culpa" ("The wickedness of the act in true delicts is malice, in quasi-delicts it is negligence"). (See also his 4.5.1.) Giambattista de Luca (1614–1683), discussing delicts in *Instituta universale di Tutte le Leggi* (4.2,3,4,5 §1), said, "oggi in pratica resta più comoda l'azione Criminale" ("today in practice the criminal action is more helpful"). He even claimed (at §7) that it was not worthwhile to spend time on the action of the *lex Aquilia,* which was rarely used.

The main Roman delicts were *furtum* (theft), *rapina* (robbery with violence), *damnum iniuria datum* (wrongful damage to property), and *iniuria* (which covered both defamation and physical assault). In later law (if not also in Roman law), all of these were covered above all by criminal law, because with the sole exception of *damnum iniuria datum* they all required deliberate malicious conduct on the part of the malefactor. For *damnum iniuria datum*, the wrongful action had to be either malicious or simply negligent. In Western Europe in the later Middle Ages, specific difficulties hindered the Reception of the Roman law of delict. In France, there was no Reception of the Roman law.[35] The tragedy for France was that in excluding *delicta* from discussion as being above all crimes and as being law that was not received, the French writers also deprived themselves of a treatment of the *lex Aquilia*,[36] since that is the context in Roman law in which one finds the treatment par excellence of negligence in all its aspects and of negligent injury to things and human beings. (Injury to human beings comes under *damnum iniuria datum* because slaves were a prime kind of property, and to a great extent dependent children in law could be analogized to slaves.) Hence, subsequent treatment by the jurists who took this approach is weak regarding the basis of liability for tortious wrongdoing.

Domat discusses liability for things poured or thrown out of windows or dangerously suspended, but there is no other case of liability for injury proceeding from an inanimate movable thing or from a person's wrongful act except in the most general terms and without analysis (as in book 2, title 8, section 4). Pothier says not a word on the basis of liability for damage by a thing, and in the discussions before the Conseil d'Etat concerning the draft of the *code civil* no time was spent on the meaning of "dommage . . . causé par le fait . . . des choses que l'on a sous sa garde." Significantly, the draft contained two other specific articles that would have appeared immediately after the existing art. 1381:

Art. 16. If, from a house inhabited by several persons, water or something which causes damage is thrown onto a passerby, those who inhabit the apartment from which it was thrown are all liable in solidarity, unless he who did the throwing is known, in which case he alone has the obligation of restoring the loss.

Art. 17. Guests who only inhabit in passing the house from which the thing was thrown are not bound to repair the loss, unless it has been proved that it was they who threw; but he who lodges them is bound.[37]

14

These two draft articles have supreme significance for under-standing the drafting of this part of the *code civil*. They both relate only to the circumstances of the Roman *actio de effusis vel deiectis*, and they both concern particular situations: where there is more than one principal inhabitant and where the inhabitants are tem-porary guests. As particular cases, they illuminate the main notion and reveal the context of the discussion. Art. 16 was at first accepted without discussion in the Conseil d'Etat, but in discussing art. 17, Citizen Miot claimed that the enunciation of the principle sufficed and that examples should be cut back.[38] Not a word was said in the Conseil d'Etat regarding liability for damage by things under what is now art. 1384. Likewise, when that part of the *code* was presented before the Corps législatif on 19 February 1804, not a word on the subject was spoken by Treilhard in his presentation or by the tribun Tarrible in its discussion.[39]

Indeed until the importance of the rule showed up in practice, liability for damage caused by things attracted little scholarly atten-tion. For instance, the long-winded commentator on the code, Toul-lier, who devoted twenty-one articles to a discussion of damage by animals, gave only one to damage caused by inanimate objects—and that, after a brief mention of art. 1384, is devoted to art. 1386.[40] Likewise, even as late as 1877, F. Mourlon in his published lectures on the *code civil* dealt under art. 1384 only with persons for whom one is responsible, and under the heading of things under one's guard only with arts. 1385 and 1386.[41] Indeed, so little was made of liability concerning things under one's guard in the debates, so little attention was paid to it in practice before the Teffaine case of 1896,[42] and so obscure is the background to the clause, that it can be said to be the unanimous opinion in France that the drafters' intention was to establish liability only for animals and collapsing buildings, and that the relevant part of art. 1384 simply announced the particular cases in arts. 1385 and 1386.[43]

But we cannot leave art. 1384 yet. We must still consider some aspects of liability for the acts of persons for whom one is respon-sible. Domat says in *Les Lois Civiles* (1.2.8.7.): "Schoolmasters, craftsmen and others who receive into their homes students, ap-prentices or other persons to train them in some art, manufacture or commerce are liable for the behavior of these people."[44] We have here an early statement regarding liability for other persons' behavior in French law. As it stands, removed from its context, it has no parallel in Roman law. In Roman law, one was responsible for the conduct of one's slaves and sons-in-power, not for pupils, apprentices, and others whom one was training. But the context is important for Domat. The text arises out of the discussion of things poured or thrown out of windows and probably should be restricted to that (for Domat), though no restriction is expressed. Then there would be absolute liability in Roman law, and Domat expresses the liability in absolute terms. Interestingly, Domat cites in support D.9.3.5.3, which in fact has a rather different effect. What is at issue there is who is to be regarded as a *habitator*, inhabitant, and the text indicates that an action on the facts will be given if one hires a building to have work done there or to teach pupils there (and one does not sleep there) and damage ensues.

The issue is taken up again by Pothier, who asserts that one is also liable for the acts of persons subject to one's power, as fathers, mothers, tutors, and teachers when the delict or quasi-delict is committed in one's presence, and generally when one could have prevented the injury but did not. But if one could not have prevented it, there is no liability. Pothier adds that one is liable for the wrongs caused by servants and employees even when one could not prevent the wrong, provided the wrong was committed in the exercise of the functions for which the servants or employees were employed.[45] This brings us closer to the rules set out in the *code civil*. For Bertrand de Greuille, addressing the Tribunat on 6 February 1803, teachers and craftsmen were responsible for the acts of their pupils and apprentices, because they took the place of the parents—not at all the Roman position.[46]

The line of historical development from Domat is fairly plain. He stated absolutely the liability for pupils and such others (and this was proper in its context). Pothier generalized this approach, whether he had Domat or an equivalent statement in his mind. But in a general context the liability had to be restricted—to wrongs that the parent or teacher could not have prevented. And then Pothier added his treatment of liability for servants and employees. But, as was said before, the basis of one's liability for the acts of children, pupils, and apprentices had consequently become stricter in the *code civil* than the basis of liability for one's own acts. The main reasons for this lie first in the removal from the French discussion of any treatment of the *lex Aquilia*, where the principle of no liability without fault is laid out, with the consequent blurring in French law of this all-important principle. The second reason lies in Domat's unqualified statement of absolute liability (but in the limited context of the *actio de effusis vel deiectis*), and Pothier's having had before him some discussion such as Domat's to which he added qualifications (untrammeled by too much consideration of the *lex Aquilia*). Third, Pothier's views were adopted by the code commission without too much evidence of independent thought.

For art. 1385, the *travaux préparatoires* make the best starting point for the long answer, since the codifiers' intent there is readily apparent. Treilhard said nothing in the Conseil d'Etat, but Bertrand de Greuille was explicit:

> The draft then considers the cases where an animal, led by someone or escaped from his hands or having simply wandered off, has caused some wrong. In the first two hypotheses, the draft intends that the person who uses the animal, and in the third it orders the person who is its owner to be held liable for the reparation of the loss, because the loss must be imputed either to a lack of guard and vigilance on the part of the master, or to the rashness, clumsiness or lack of attention of him who used the animal and because, in addition, within the general thesis, nothing belonging to someone can injure another with impunity.[47]

Thus for de Greuille, the liability of the owner or user of the animal was absolute, and he had two basic arguments. The first is one of imputed fault, and the second is that liability for animals falls within the general category of liability for things (under art. 1384), and that liability is absolute. Tarrible's remarks are shorter but base liability on negligence that, however, may be very slight.[48] Thus, there seems to be some conflict regarding the interpretation of the article, even among the legislators. But Bertrand de Greuille is the more explicit and his intention was to establish absolute liability for the acts of animals. This would correspond very accurately to the three remedies of Roman law if one assumed that the *actio de pastu* was not limited to the situation in which the owner sent his animals to feed on another's land and thus that the action would be noxal. Domat certainly takes this broad view of the *actio de pastu*, though he says nothing about noxal surrender. This is in keeping with the approach that he says he is taking with regard to damage by animals; since customs varied so much, he set down only general rules that might be of common use, not what was particular to local customs or what was contained in Roman law but not in those customs (hence he does not deal with noxal surrender).[49] In fact what he gives is Roman law, with omissions.[50] There is again in this context no recourse by the drafters to local customary law, though customary law was extensive, especially with regard to pasturage.[51] Here, too, the formulation of art. 1385 can be said to be the result of Domat's treatment, which was based on Roman law. From this, however, was excised noxal surrender, which had given the Roman rules a different impact.[52]

To establish the connection here concerning liability under art. 1386 for the collapse of a building and the very different remedies for *damnum infectum* in Roman law, we need do nothing more now than consider the remarks of Bertrand de Greuille in the Conseil d'Etat:[53]

> It is also as a consequence of that incontestable truth that the last article of the draft holds that the owner of a building is responsible for the loss which it caused by its collapse when that occurred through defective maintenance or by a flaw in its construction. This decision is much less rigorous and more equitable than the provision which is found in Roman law. That authorized the individual whose building could be damaged by the fall of another which was in danger of collapse, to put himself in possession of this neighboring heritage, if the proprietor did not give him guarantees for the loss one had reason to fear. Thus apprehension of the harm itself gave an opening for the action, and could bring the dispossession into play: the draft to the contrary intends above all that the harm be present. It is thus the collapse alone which can legitimate the complaint and the demand of the injured party, and determine a condemnation for his benefit. It is after this collapse that he is allowed to examine the injury, to decide its importance; and it is then that the judge gives a decision on its reparation, if it is established that the negligence of the owner in maintaining his building or the ignorance of the workmen whom he employed in its construction were the cause of the collapse.[54]

Thus, Bertrand de Greuille expressly links liability under art. 1386 with the very different Roman remedies for *damnum infectum*. Whether the Roman remedies were or were not less equitable need not concern us. What does matter is a feature that was inappropriately carried over, to a different effect, and which made imbalanced the French liability for wrongful damage. The Roman remedy was given for threatened future damage. That means that the future collapse was apparent if nothing were done; for the owner then to do nothing to prevent the collapse would in fact be negligence. This would be so even when the defect arose from a fault in construction. But the French action was for past damage and was given even for a fault in the construction that was unknown to the owner. Thus, French liability came to differ from liability in Roman law. More than that, liability under art. 1386 differs from liability under arts. 1382 and 1383 in not requiring negligence and from 1384 in requiring a defect in the thing (in the absence of negligence).

The obduracy of the inappropriate Roman *damnum infectum* clearly appears when we examine the 24 November 1803 discussion in the Conseil d'Etat and notice that Regnaud wanted to excise the offending "par une suite du défaut d'entretien ou par le vice de la construction" ("in consequence of defective maintenance or by a flaw in the construction") and substitute "par sa faute" ("through his fault"). This attempt to make liability depend on fault was rejected.[55]

With these five articles on wrongful damage in the French *code civil*, we are thus face to face with a very complex and peculiar phenomenon in legal development. They do not at all harmonize on the subject of the basis of legal liability. This does not seem to be the result of careful thought on the different situations by the legislators, nor simply the result of poor draftsmanship. Rather, it is the outcome of past legal history and above all the consequence of a reliance on a discussion of liability largely in the context of inappropriate Roman law, which had been rejected in large measure. There was no recourse to the rules of customary law. One can say that Roman law here was not received, but it nonetheless was the initial factor—and the dominant factor—in determining the shape of the French rules in the *code civil*.

To avoid misunderstanding, there is one point that ought to be made explicit. I am, of course, not claiming that there is no place for different standards of liability to operate in different situations for wrongful injury. Nor am I claiming that the French rules were necessarily grotesque for the French in 1804. But I am claiming that the various bases of liability in the French articles were adopted, without much thought or social purpose, from rejected Roman originals of which traces survived in old French books, and that the drafting, based as it was on preconceptions deriving from the old works, failed to achieve clarity. A glance at the corresponding articles in the German *Bürgerliches Gesetzbuch* (*BGB*) §§823 to 853—themselves much influenced by Roman law—or, for the United States, at any edition of *Prosser on Torts*, will show that very different rules could just as easily have been accepted.

These rules of the *code civil* illustrate a proposition that I regard as being of the highest importance and that is already inherent in past work of mine. The proposition is that in any country, approaches to lawmaking (whether by legislators, judges, or jurists), the applicability of law to social institutions, the structure of the legal system, the formulation and scope of legal rules, are all in very large measure the result of past history and overwhelmingly the result of past legal history, and that the input of other, even contemporary societal forces is correspondingly slight. Thus, for instance, to understand why a piece of legislation or a judicial decision is as it is, we must know the legal tradition within which the lawmakers operate. And, given the prevalence and importance of legal borrowing and the ancient roots of much of law, this means that, to a very great extent, attitudes toward lawmaking, the structure of legal systems, the parameters of legal rules, and the outlook of lawyers can be explained only if we examine the law in its historical relation to other law and over a period of centuries.

One final problem should be considered. Art. 1382 reads: "Tout fait quelconque de l'homme, qui cause à autrui un dommage, oblige celui par la faute duquel il est arrivé, a le réparer." *Fait* may reasonably be translated as "action" and in itself does not seem to carry a connotation of blame or of wrongful action. The wrong that gives rise to an action is denoted by *faute*, or fault, a word that does not necessarily imply deliberate wrongdoing. But art. 1383 reads: "Chacun est responsable du dommage qu'il a causé, non seulement par son fait, mais encore par sa négligence ou par son imprudence."

If we take "fait" in this article also to mean action and not to connote blameworthiness, then "par sa négligence ou par son imprudence," appearing in contrast to it, should mean that one is also liable for not acting and should denote a liability for nonfeasance even when there was no affirmative duty to act. "Négligence" is not contrasted with "dol." Art. 1383 has "fait," not even "faute," which, in a pinch, to give a proper sense to "négligence" one might even want to translate as "deliberate wrong." Yet we know from the *travaux préparatoires*[56] that it was not the intention to give an action for nonfeasance, but rather to make clear that the action for wrongful loss existed both when there was malice and also when there was merely negligence. Thus, art. 1383 was poorly drafted. But what, in any event, is the point of having these two articles? Why not simply have one reading: "Tout fait quelconque de l'homme, qui cause à autrui un dommage, oblige celui par le dol ou la négligence ou l'imprudence duquel il est arrivé, a le réparer." The answer lies in a previous French distortion of Roman law. As early as Pothier, a sharp distinction was made: a "délit" was a wrongful act done maliciously; a "quasi-délit" was a wrongful act done negligently.[57] The point—unexpressed—of art. 1383 was to indicate that a negligent act that causes harm also creates liability.[58]

But these lectures are dedicated to failures of the legal imagination. Whose imagination failed? Not obviously, I think, that of the Roman jurists. Certainly, that of Domat, in treating all *delicta* as crimes when he need not have done so. Even if he did not wish to discuss the *lex Aquilia*, he could have made use of the Roman discussion of negligence and liability. By failing to include the basic scenarios of damage caused by someone responsible for his or her own behavior, Domat lost the emphasis on the basic framework of liability only for fault including negligence; the exceptional cases were not fitted into the scheme of things with their rationales and boundaries explained. Subsequent French jurists, like Pothier, in following such a model also failed to set out an adequate treatment of private wrongs. A considerable failure of the imagination must be attributed to the drafters of the *code civil*, who seem to have been blithely unaware of the inconsistencies in the articles and of the history of the rules they were perpetuating, especially since they stood at the point at which satisfactory law most easily might have been made.

But failures of the legal imagination have consequences: they entail future failures. Law has practical effects, but, as I have argued elsewhere,[59] it has to a very considerable degree a life of its own. Law has functions related to the practical life, but it also operates at the level of culture, especially regarding the culture of the lawmaking elite, which has the power to make changes in the law. And a living culture is not examined by those who live it. Three typical features of law as culture are pertinent to the present failure of legal imagination, though none will be examined here in depth. First, codified legal rules are resistant to removal or replacement. Second, society and lawyers on a day-to-day basis can tolerate much inappropriate, even absurd, law. Third, legal rules, when available in an accessible form, can readily be borrowed often without an inquiry into their effectiveness.

With regard to the first feature, four of the five articles remain unchanged in the current French *code civil*, though there has been subsequent relevant legislation. Art. 1384 has undergone modification but mainly with regard to liability for persons for whom one is responsible, and for things under one's guard, though only in minor respects.

With regard to the second feature, we should perhaps talk less of a failure of the legal imagination than of an excess of the legal imagination. S. F. C. Milsom has well stated the issue for the history of English common law:

> The life of the common law has been in the abuse of its elementary ideas. If the rules of property give now what seems an unjust answer, try obligation; and equity has proved that from the materials of obligation you can counterfeit the phenomena of property. If the rules of contract give what now seems an unjust answer, try tort. Your counterfeit will look odd to one brought up on categories of Roman origin; but it will work. If the rules of one tort, say deceit, give what now seems an unjust answer, try another, try negligence. And so the legal world goes round.[60]

Much of Milsom's book, however, serves to demonstrate that though the counterfeits (as he calls them) work, they do not work well; and often indeed the counterfeits cannot be created at the right time. In France, arts. 1382 and 1383 have always been interpreted as meaning that for one's own act, liability was based on fault that the victim-plaintiff had to prove. At first, liability for animals under art. 1385 was based on fault that was presumed but, by the late nineteenth century, liability was strict and the owner or the person using the animal was liable unless he could show *force majeure*, the act of a third party or the fault of the victim. Interpretation of art. 1386 has been reasonably stable: if a building collapsed,[61] the owner was not excused from liability just because he established that he was free from fault, for example if he had charged a competent builder with the maintenance of the building or if it was humanly impossible to uncover the defect. The greatest variation in interpretation—desperate attempts to make some social sense of the provision—has occurred with regard to liability under art. 1384 for things under one's guard. The range of interpretations has been enormous and will not be examined here, but it has swung from liability only if the keeper could be shown to be at fault, through liability if the thing was defective even if this was not known to the keeper, through strict liability that can be rebutted only if the keeper proves *cas fortuit, force majeure,* or a *cause étrangère* that cannot be imputed to him. It has even been held that when a thing in motion (such as an automobile) is under the control of the keeper, the keeper is liable under art. 1384 for damage caused by the thing (even when it is not defective) unless he can show *cas fortuit, force majeure,* or *cause étrangère.* Under this interpretation, an automobile driver may be liable without fault under art. 1384, ignoring arts. 1382 and 1383.[62]

As to the third typical feature of law as culture—the easy transplanting of rules without an inquiry into their effectiveness—we can even make a random choice of examples. Thus, the *code civil* for the lands of the king of Sardinia of 1837 gives the French provisions verbatim.[63] The Dominican Republic took over the *code civil* in 1845 and translated it into Spanish only in 1884; the French provisions remain unaltered to the present day as arts. 1382 to 1386 of the *codigo civil.* The Italian *codice civile* of 1865 simply translated the French articles as arts. 1151 to 1155 but with the addition of art. 1156 fixing liability *in solidum* if several persons were liable for the delict or quasi-delict.

I wish to clarify what I am claiming from the example of arts.

1382 to 1386. I am not asserting that the French *code civil* is nothing but a modernized version of Roman law—the articles themselves show that much was not received—nor am I claiming that the explanation of each article of the *code civil* is to be found in Roman law. I am claiming that the articles of the *code*—and I would extend this to all legislation, I think—can be fully understood with regard both to their form and their substance only if there is an inquiry into the cultural history behind them, and this inquiry must often span centuries and countries. I would also claim that the force of a Reception, in this case of Roman law, is not to be judged simply by the acceptance of rules and structures, but by the extent of dependence on a foreign system.

Arts. 1382 to 1386 do not stand alone in this regard. I should like to mention only a few other oddities in the French *code civil* without, however, detailing their history. The first paragraph of art. 1110 reads: "Error is not a cause of nullity of the agreement unless it falls upon the very substance of the thing which is its object."[64] The meaning of "substance" is not further clarified and is the subject of much doubt. Scholars likewise dispute the obscure *error in substantia* in Roman law, its meaning, its acceptance by jurists, and its scope.[65] The model or models for the French drafters are not apparent nor is their intention. The article in the *projet*, art. 8 of "Du Consentement," was accepted in the Conseil d'Etat without discussion on 11 Brumaire, an 12 (1803).[66] In explaining the reasons for the article in the *code* before the Conseil d'Etat, Bigot-Préameneu, after mentioning "la substance même de la chose," said:

> It is by following this rule that one must decide with Barbeyrac and Pothier that error in the motivation of the agreement is only a cause of nullity in the case where the accuracy of these motifs can be regarded as a condition on which it is clear that the parties intended their contract to depend.[67]

And Mouricault said: "It is necessary that the error bore on the very substance of the thing or on the motive which determined the agreement," and he referred to Pothier twice in the immediately succeeding discussion.[68] Likewise, Favard, though he is less explicit regarding the meaning of "substance," cites Pothier in the connected context of the avoidance of contract because of fraud or force.[69] And subsequent commentators[70] and judges have considered Pothier's views to be very relevant in the interpretation of the article. But it must be doubtful if Pothier's formulation was immediately before the eyes of the *projet's* drafters. Pothier wrote: "Error avoids the agreement, not only when it is as to the thing itself, but also when it is as to the quality of the thing which the parties had principally in mind, and which constitutes the substance of that thing."[71]

Pothier thus clarified the notion of substance, giving it a meaning it never had in Roman law. Although it can be assumed that the French codifiers intended to follow Pothier's view, the absence from art. 1110 of anything resembling his formulation of the meaning of substance suggests that they had a simpler model before them, such as perhaps G. Argou, *Institution au droit françois:* "With respect to error, that only vitiates the contract of sale when it is met with in regard to the substance of the bought thing."[72] In the seventeenth and eighteenth centuries, throughout Europe there were many books like Argou's that one might term "Institutes of local law," and which in their arrangement and subject matter had their foundations in Justinian's *Institutes.* French books of the institutional type seem to have had a strong influence on the structure of the *code civil.*[73] Thus, we have here another, but simpler, instance of a Reception of Roman law in which the Roman rules were rejected. The compilers presumably followed the opinion of Pothier, which was not that of any Roman jurist. But Pothier retained the use of the Roman terminology, "substance," and some later writers, like those of the institutes, did not expound on the nature of error with regard to substance. Lack of clarity as to the meaning of the simple-sounding *code* provision ensued. There were at least two failures of the legal imagination—of Pothier, in retaining the Roman terminology (at least when he was not much more explicit as to the extent that his theory diverged from the Roman), and of the codifiers, in failing to see the full ambiguity of the word *substance,* given its past history.

Another example could be the famous doctrine of "cause." Art. 1131 reads "The obligation without cause, or on a false cause or on an illicit cause, can have no effect."[74]

We do not need to say much here, since the story is well known.

As is agreed, the modern idea does not appear in Roman law or in early French law.[75] *Causa* does, of course, make its appearance in the Roman legal sources, but its role in the field of obligations is ambiguous at best. *D.2.14.7.4* tells us that when there is no *causa* there is no obligation on account of agreement. And *D.15.1.49.2* reads to the effect that whether a master is debtor to his slave or vice versa is to be computed *ex causa civili. Causa* appears more prominently as a basis for acquisition of ownership by delivery or prescription.[76]

In French law, the notion basically goes back to Domat (though there are canon law forerunners),[77] who set out a precise scheme, with contracts divided into types: bilateral, unilateral but for a consideration, and gifts.[78] Pothier was rather less explicit,[79] the discussions of the article in the Conseil d'Etat were not a little confused,[80] and art. 1131 lacks all clarity on the meaning of *"cause."* Not surprisingly, the early commentators called attention to the obscurity of art. 1131.[81] More recent writers have concentrated their efforts not only on defining and refining the nature of cause but also on discovering its practical value and theoretical validity. Though it seems likely to retain some place in French law, cause, for many French legal writers and for more outsiders, is thought to have little practical value and to be theoretically incorrect and unnecessary.[82] At the very least, there would, I think, be general agreement that the practical importance of cause has often been grossly exaggerated and that theoretically its significance is difficult to explain. But, as the treatment in Domat and others shows, it obviously is another example where Roman law rules were not accepted but formed the basis of discussion in French law until codification,[83] and to some extent influenced the later rules.

What I have been concerned with here is above all legal rules and their formation, not law in action, not how in lawsuits or administrative dealings the law can be manipulated for the benefit of particular individuals or groups. And it must be admitted by all, I think, that though law in action may differ from law in books, law in books has, at the very least, a very powerful effect on how law can be manipulated in practice.

Law in books then. It is extremely significant that both the legislators of Napoleonic France and powerful academic theorists of earlier ages were so little interested in the impact of the rules of delict on particular groups or in the social effect of the rules concerning the basis of liability. The rules were taken over, with no apparent interest in their effect, from ancient roots from which some parts have been chopped. Admittedly, the legislators at times used language such as "nothing belonging to someone else can injure another with impunity," but this seems intended to be a justification of a predetermined rule, not an argument toward a rule.

With liability for things under one's guard under art. 1384, there is undoubtedly social awareness among both professors and judges in their interpretations. But there is also a legal culture, as the cases indicate. An interpretation, whether of judges or professors, becomes established and may remain stable for years, despite a failure to achieve the social result sought by those who originally favored the interpretation.

There is thus an underlying theme in this chapter: the legal tradition, as an intellectual, cultural force, plays an extremely important but largely unrecognized role in lawmaking—even in legislation and even at a time when a new beginning is stressed. Legal rules, even in legislation, have an intellectual, dogmatic history, not just a social, political, or economic history. Law is not an end in itself but can only be a means to an end. Yet often the end or ends to which the law is a means do not stand clearly before the eyes of the lawmakers.[84]

Moreover, as I shall argue more fully in Chapter 5, legal academics, too, are often so blinded by the tradition in which they work that they misconceive what they are doing. Thus, it is not particularly surprising to find modern French scholars claiming that certain applications of the *lex Aquilia* can be explained according to the modern theory of risk. Still it is offputting to find the same scholars declaring that the Roman praetorian edict *de effusis vel deiectis* can only be explained by the theory of risk, by responsibility for the acts of things under one's guard (art. 1384), while they show no awareness that liability for things under art. 1384 derives from that edict.[85]

NOTES TO CHAPTER 1

1. See in general, Coing, *Privatrecht*, 1. On proliferation of courts in Germany, see G. Strauss, *Law, Resistance and the State* (Princeton, N.J.: Princeton University Press, 1986), p. 122. In this present book, the terms *private law* and *public law* appear frequently. I am fully aware that the distinction is not easy to draw, that many legal rules or statutes partake of both, and that, especially for medieval law (though also at other times), the distinction has little substance. But, as many others have found, the distinction is, in general, a convenient one. My usage of "private law" is, I hope, consistent as well as useful: the term covers all those topics of law that are dealt with in the *Institutes* of Justinian, with the exception of crimes and actions: precisely the subject matter of modern civil codes.

2. To see the impact of this undervaluation of local customary law, it is enough to examine Coing, *Privatrecht*, 1, and the volumes produced under his guidance: Coing, *Handbuch*.

3. For an account of the impact of sophisticated law in writing on customary legal systems see Watson, *Evolution*, pp. 66ff.

4. See *General Survey of Events, Sources, Persons and Movements in Continental Legal History*, by various European authors (Boston: Little, Brown, 1912), p. 286.

5. *Histoire du droit civil français*, 3rd ed. (Paris, 1905), p. 220. Viollet would not refuse some place to Roman law; see *Histoire*, pp. 11ff.

6. *Comparative Law*, 4th ed. (Mineola, N.Y.: Foundation Press, 1980), p. 280.

7. 1382. Tout fait quelconque de l'homme, qui cause à autrui un dommage, oblige celui par la faute duquel il est arrivé, à le réparer.

1383. Chacun est responsable du dommage qu'il a causé, non seulement par son fait, mais encore par sa négligence ou par son imprudence.

1384. On est responsable, non seulement du dommage que l'on cause par son propre fait, mais encore de celui qui est causé par le fait des personnes dont on doit répondre, ou des choses que l'on a sous sa garde.

Le père, et la mère après le décès du mari, sont responsables du dommage causé par leurs enfans mineurs habitant avec eux;

Les maîtres et les commettans, du dommage causé par leurs domestiques et préposés dans les functions auxquelles il les ont employés;

Les instituteurs et les artisans, du dommage causé par leurs élèves et apprentis pendant le temps qu'ils sont sous leur surveillance.

La responsabilité ci-dessus a lieu, à moins que les père et mère, instituteurs et artisans, ne prouvent qu'ils n'ont pu empêcher le fait qui donne lieu à cette responsabilité.

1385. Le propriétaire d'un animal, ou celui qui s'en sert, pendant qu'il est à son usage, est responsable du dommage que l'animal a causé soit que l'animal fût sous sa garde, soit qu'il fût égaré ou échappé.

1386. Le propriétaire d'un bâtiment est responsable du dommage causé par sa ruine, lorsqu'elle est arrivée par une suite du défaut d'entretien ou par le vice de la construction.

8. See, for example, A. Weill and F. Terré, *Droit civil: introduction générale*, 4th ed. (Paris: Dalloz, 1979), p. 184.

9. The terms *délit* and *quasi-délit* do appear in art. 1370, along with *quasi-contrat* as types of obligations that arise without agreement, but they are neither defined nor explained.

10. See, for example, *D.9.2.*

11. See, for example, *D*.9.2.27.3; *h.t.* 32*pr.*; *h.t.* 44.1; 9.4.2 *pr.*, 1; *h.t.* 4.2; *h.t.* 6.

12. The rules are complicated and of no consequence here, but see, for example, Watson, *Obligations*, pp. 274ff.

13. See *D*.9.3.

14. See, above all, *D*.9.3.1.4.

15. *D*.9.3.1.4.

16. See *D*.9.3.5.6 ff.

17. I believe that the occupier was liable only if he placed or knew of the placing of the object: "Liability in the *actio de positis ac suspensis*"; *Mélanges Philippe Meylan*, 1, (Lausanne: Imprimerie Centrale de Lausanne, 1963), pp. 379ff. My view and its accuracy are irrelevant in the present context, where what matters is the traditional view that the occupier was liable even without fault.

18. See *D*.9.1

19. See *D*.10.4.9.1; *D*.19.5.14.3.

20. See *Pauli Sententiae*, 1.15.1; also see Lenel, *Edictum*, p. 198.

21. *D*.21.1.40; *h.t.* 41; *h.t.* 42.

22. *Les Lois Civiles*, 2.7.3.

23. Fenet, *Travaux préparatoires*, 13, p. 477.

24. See, for example, *D*.39.2.7.1,2.

25. See, for example, *D*.39.2.24.4-11; *h.t.* 43*pr.*

26. We need not go into details; see, for example, Kaser, *Privatrecht*, 1, pp. 408f.

27. There were a few other special remedies, such as the *actio aquae pluviae arcendae*, the action for warding off rain water.

28. *D*.39.2.24.9.

29. See, above all, Lenel, *Edictum*, p. 551.

30. But French case law has held that art. 1386 also applied to damage from defective trees: see Cour d'Appel, Paris, Première Chambre, 20.8.1877; S.1878 II.48.

31. *Traité des Lois*, 13.9.

32. See the first paragraph of his preface to *Les Lois Civiles*.

33. On peut distinguer trois sortes de fautes dont il peut arriver quelque dommage: celles qui vont à un crime ou à un délit; celles des personnes qui manquent aux engagèmens des conventions, comme un vendeur qui ne délivre pas la chose vendue, un locataire qui ne fait pas les réparations dont il est tenu; et celles qui n'ont point de rapport aux conventions, et qui ne vont pas à un crime ni à un délit, comme si par légèreté on jette quelque chose par une fenêtre qui gâte un habit: si des animaux mal gardés font quelque dommage; si on cause un incendie par une imprudence, si un bâtiment qui menace ruine, n'étant pas réparé, tombe sur un autre, et y fait du dommage.

De ces trois sortes de fautes, il n'y a que celles de la dernière espèce qui soient la matière de ce titre; car les crimes et les délits ne doivent pas être mêlés avec les matières civiles, et tout ce qui regarde les conventions, a été expliqué dans le premier livre.

34. See 1.1.2.2.

35. See, for example, C. de Ferrière, *La Jurisprudence du Digeste* (1677), on *D*.9.2; cf. A. Dumas, *Histoire des Obligations dans l'Ancien Droit français* (Aix-en-Provence: Faculté de Droit et de Science Politique, 1972), p. 33; Coing, *Privatrecht*, 1, pp. 504ff.

36. There were other reasons for neglecting the *lex Aquilia*, because it could well be doubted whether that statute had been "received" into later law. See the discussion

of the opinions of Christianus Thomasius (1655–1728) and J. H. Heineccius (1681–1741) in Watson, *Transplants*, pp. 79ff.

37. Art. 16. Si, d'une maison habitée par plusieurs personnes, il est jeté sur un passant de l'eau, ou quelque chose qui cause un dommage, ceux qui habitent l'appartement d'où on l'a jeté sont tous solidairement responsables, à moins que celui qui a jeté ne soit connu, auquel cas il doit seul la réparation du dommage.

Art. 17. Les hôtes qui n'habitent qu'en passant la maison d'où la chose a été jetée, ne soit point tenus de la réparation du dommage, à moins qu'il ne soit prouvé que ce sont eux qui ont jeté; mais celui qui les loge en est tenu.

38. *Procès-Verbaux*, 3, pp. 311ff. Cf. C.-B.-M. Toullier, *Le Droit civil Français*, 11, 5th ed. (Paris, 1830), pp. 192f.; C. Baudry-Lacantinerie and L. Barde, *Traité Théorique et Pratique de Droit Civil, Les Obligations*, 4, 3rd ed. (Paris: Sirey, 1908), pp. 653f.

39. See Fenet, *Travaux préparatoires*, 13, pp. 464ff.

40. Toullier, *Le Droit civil*, pp. 433ff.; cf., e.g., the remarks of A. Tunc, "A Codified Law of Tort—The French Experience," *Louisiana Law Review* 39 (1979): 1051ff.

41. F. Mourlon, *Répétitions écrites sur le code civil contenant l'exposé des principes généraux*, 2 (Paris, 1877), pp. 892ff., especially at 895. The same silence is observed by V. Marcadé, *Explication théorique et pratique du code Napoléon*, 5 (Paris, 1859), pp. 267ff.; J.-B.-C. Picot, *Code Napoléon expliqué article par article* (Paris, n.d.), pp. 58ff.; A. Duranton, *Cours de droit civil*, 7, 4th ed. (Brussels, 1841), pp. 508ff. The same is true for the famous work of C. S. Zachariae, *Cours de droit civil français*, revu et augmenté par C. Aubry et C. Rau, 3 (Strasbourg, 1839), pp. 202f., and also A. M. Demante with E. Colmet de Santerre, *Cours analytique de Code civil*, 5, 2nd ed. (Paris, 1883), pp. 660ff. The explication of Bosquet is illuminating. On art. 1384 he writes: "Les choses qu'on a sous sa garde sont mobilières ou immobilières, elles sont sans vie ou avec vie. Ce ne peut être que du fait de ces dernières, dont le présent article a entendu parler. Mais, dans cette acceptation, l'article 1385 n'est-il pas suffisant?" ("Things which one has under one's guard are movable or immovable, they are inanimate or animate. The present article can have intended to speak only of those last named. But, with this understanding, is article 1385 not sufficient?") *Explication du code civil* 3 (Avignon, 1805).

42. S.1897.1.17 (to be found in English in A. T. von Mehren and J. R. Gordley, *The Civil Law System*, 2nd ed. [Boston: Little, Brown, 1977], pp. 608ff.).

43. See G. Viney, *Les Obligations, La Responsabilité: Conditions* (Paris: L.G.D.J., 1982: in the series *Traité de Droit Civil*, directed by J. Ghastin), p. 749. In the case of Jand'heur c. Galéries Belfortaises, P. Matter claimed that liability for things under one's guard derived from old French customary law; see Dalloz, *Recueil Périodique et Critique* 1 (1930): 65.

44. "Les maîtres d'école, les artisans et autres qui reçoivent dans leurs maisons des écoliers, apprentis, ou d'autres personnes pour quelque art, quelque manufacture ou quelque commerce, sont tenus du fait de ces personnes."

45. The idea had already appeared in practice that an employer was liable for loss caused by the fault or clumsiness of mule drivers, carters, or coachmen; see C. de Ferrière, *Jurisprudence*, on *D.9.2*.

46. Reported in Locré, *Législation* 13, p. 42.

47. Le projet prévoit ensuite les cas ou un animal guidé par quelqu'un, ou échappé de ses mains, ou simplement égaré, aurait causé quelque tort. Dans les deux premières hypothèses, il veut que celui qui s'en servait, et dans la troisième, il ordonne que celui qui en est le propriétaire soit tenu de la réparation du dommage, parce qu'alors ce dommage doit être imputé, soit au défaut de garde et de vigilance de la part du maître, soit à la témérité, à la maladresse ou au peu d'attention de celui qui s'est servi de l'animal, et parce que d'ailleurs dans la thèse générale rien de ce qui appartient à quelqu'un ne peut nuire impunément à un autre. Quoted from Locré, *Législation* 13, p. 43.

48. Locré, *Législation* 13, p. 58.

49. *Les Lois Civiles*, 1.2.7.2.

50. However, although he bases his idea on Roman law authority, he seems to hold that for the *actio de pauperie*, in some situations at least, liability depends on the owner's knowing about his animal's bad habits and still not taking care; see Ibid., 1.2.7.2.6,7,8.

51. For a few examples chosen almost at random, see Guy Coquille, *Conférence des Coustumes de France* (Paris, 1642), p. 211; *Coustumes générales de Berry*, title 10, art. 1–4 (pasturage); *Coustumes générales du bailliage de Troyes*, art. 118 (wandering animals); art. 121, arts. 167–172 (pasturage), *Coustumes de Melun*, arts. 302–309 (pasturage); M. Petitjean and M. L. Marchand, *Le Coutumier Bourguignon glosé* (Paris, CNRS, 1982), pp. 232, §273, 239 §300 (delict), pp. 32 §3, 236 §287, 291 §402. Interestingly, despite the practical importance of damage by animals, nothing is said on the subject by writers such as A. Loysel, *Institutes Coutumières* (first published in 1607) or G. Argou, *Institution au Droit françois* (first published in 1692). Very different, though, is de Ferrière, *Jurisprudence*, on D.9.1.

52. This last sentence may perhaps be misleading. If Domat's treatment of responsibility for other persons was the sole *fons et origo*, then Roman noxal surrender may never have been directly relevant for subsequent French law since it has no place in the *actio de effusis vel deiectis*.

53. Treilhard said nothing à propos, and the words of Tarrible are vague but suggestive of liability only for fault (contrary to the wording of the article); see Locré, *Législation* 13, p. 58.

54. C'est encore par suite de cette incontestable vérité que le dernier article du projet décide que le propriétaire d'un bâtiment est responsable du dommage qu'il a causé par sa ruine, lorsqu'elle est arrivée par le défaut d'entretien ou par le vice de sa construction. Cette décision est bien moins rigoureuse et plus équitable que la disposition qui se trouve dans la loi romaine. Celle-ci autorisait l'individu dont le bâtiment pouvait être endommagé par la chute d'un autre qui était en péril de ruine, à se mettre en possession de cet héritage voisin, si le propriétaire ne lui donnait des sûretés pour le dommage qu'on était fondé a craindre. Ainsi la seule appréhension du mal donnait ouverture à l'action, et pouvait opérer la dépossession: le projet, au contraire, veut avant tout que le mal soit constant. C'est donc le fait seul de l'écroulement qui peut légitimer la plainte et la demande du lésé, et déterminer une condamnation à son profit. C'est après cet écroulement qu'il est permis d'examiner le dommage, de fixer son importance; et c'est alors enfin que le juge en prononce la réparation, s'il est établi que la négligence du maître à entretenir son bâtiment ou l'ignorance des ouvriers qu'il a employés à sa construction en ont déterminé la chute.

55. Fenet, *Travaux préparatoires*, 13, p. 455.

56. Locré, *Législation* 13, pp. 31, 40f., 59f.

57. *Traité des obligations*, 1.1.2.2.

58. Already J. J. Bugnet in his notes on Pothier at this point observed that the redactors of the *code* who followed Pothier seemed to intend to talk of "délits" in art. 1382 and of "quasi-délits" in art. 1383.

59. See, e.g., "Legal Change," especially from p. 1151; also see *Evolution*, pp. 115ff.

60. *Foundations*, p. 6.

61. And there must be a collapse or fall: see, e.g., M. Planiol and G. Ripert, *Traité pratique de droit civil français*, 6, *Les Obligations* (by P. Esmein) 2nd ed. (Paris: Pichon et Durand-Auzias, 1952), pp. 849f.

62. For the variety of interpretations of this part of art. 1384, see, e.g., Tunc, "A Codified Law of Tort," pp. 1064ff.; F. H. Lawson and B. S. Markesinis, *Tortious Liability for Unintentional Harm in the Common Law and Civil Law*, 1 (Cambridge: Cambridge University Press, 1982), pp. 146f. There is nothing in that work that is relevant to the argument of this chapter. For an interpretation of liability for persons for whom one is responsible under art. 1384, see, e.g., Tunc, "A Codified Law of Tort," pp. 1062ff. See also Tunc, "It is Wise Not to Take the Civil Codes Too Seriously: Traffic Accident Compensation in France," *Essays in Memory of Professor F. H. Lawson*, ed. P. Wallington and R. M. Merkin (London: Butterworths, 1980), pp. 71ff. Traffic accident law was revised by the *Loi de 5 juillet, 1985*, cf. Tunc, *Revue Internationale de Droit Comparé*, 37 (1985): 1019ff.

63. Arts. 1300–1304. Additional provisions are in arts. 1305–1307; these too have Roman law roots.

64. "L'erreur n'est une cause de nullité que lorsqu'elle tombe sur la substance même de la chose qui en est l'objet."

65. See, e.g., J. G. Wolf, *Error im römischen Vertragsrecht* (Cologne: Graz, Böhlau, 1961), especially pp. 112–165, and V. Zilletti, *La dottrina dell'errore nella storia del diritto romano* (Milan: Giuffrè, 1961), especially pp. 59–93.

66. *Procès-Verbaux* 3, p. 243.

67. Locré, *Législation* 12, p. 319.

68. Ibid., p. 554.

69. Ibid., pp. 424f.

70. See, e.g., Maleville, *Analyse Raisonné*, 13, p. 20; R. Feenstra, "The Dutch *Kantharos* case and the History of 'Error in Substantia'," *Tulane Law Review* 48 (1974): 846ff.

71. "L'erreur annule la convention, non seulement lorsqu'elle tombe sur la chose même, mais lorsqu'elle tombe sur la qualité de la chose que les contractans ont eu principalement en vue, et qui fait la substance de la chose." *Traité des obligations*, no. 18.

72. "A l'égard de l'erreur, elle ne vicie le contrat de vente, que quand elle se rencontre dans la substance de la chose achetée." 3.23.

73. For the argument that Argou's *Institution* may have provided a model for the structure of the *code civil*, see Watson, *Civil Law*, pp. 111f. P. Viollet in this connection calls attention to F. Bourjon, *Droit commun de la France et la coutume de Paris* (1747): *Histoire du droit civil français*, p. 251. See also C. Chêne, *L'Enseignement du droit français en pays de droit écrit* (Geneva: Droz, 1982), pp. 298ff.

74. "L'obligation sans cause, ou sur une fausse cause, ou sur une cause illicite, ne peut avoir aucun effet."

75. The classic modern account is in E. Gaudemet, *Théorie générale des obligations* (Paris: Sirey, 1965, a reimpression of the 1937 edition), pp. 111ff., especially at pp. 119f.

76. For an informative short statement of *causa* in Roman law, see Buckland, *Textbook of Roman Law*, 3rd ed. by P. Stein (Cambridge: Cambridge University Press, 1963), pp. 428f.

77. See, e.g., Coing, *Privatrecht*, pp. 402ff.

78. Les *Lois Civiles*, 1.1.1.5,6; 1.1.5.13.

79. *Traité des obligations*, §§ 42ff.

80. Locré, *Législation* 12, pp. 138ff.; 14, pp. 77ff.

81. See, e.g., Toullier, *Le Droit civil Français*, 6, p. 170.

82. For various accounts, see, e.g., Gaudemet, *Théorie générale*, pp. 111ff; J. Carbonnier, *Droit Civil: 4, Les Obligations*, 10th ed. (Paris: Presses Universitaires de France, 1979), pp. 106ff.: B. Nicholas, *French Law of Contract* (London: Butterworths, 1982), pp. 112ff.

83. Indeed, until later: see, e.g., Toullier, *Le Droit civil Français*, 6, p. 170.

84. I am, of course, well aware that the compilers of the *code civil* declared that absolutely new civil legislation for a great people would be above human powers, that they expressed great respect for Roman law, and that they sought a compromise between Roman law and customary law: see the "discours préliminaire" to the first *projet*, by Portalis, Tronchet, Bigot-Préameneu, and Maleville in *Conférence du Code Civil* (Paris: Firmin Didot, 1805), pp. xvii, xxxii, xxxiii.

85. P. Ourliac and J. de Malafosse, *Histoire du Droit privé, 1, Les Obligations* (Paris: Presses Universitaire de France, 1961), p. 365.

CHAPTER TWO

LEGAL EVOLUTION AND

LEGISLATION

In the first chapter, I discussed a complex case of the failure of the legal imagination that particularly concerned one example in which legislators apparently paid no attention to any social message or any clearly formulated notion of social justice in fixing the bases of liability for wrongful damage under the French *code civil*. I did not mean to suggest that the bases of liability were wildly inappropriate for early nineteenth-century France, but only that other standards could as easily have been chosen. No particular political intention determined the drafters' choice, only the impact of earlier legal writing. This impact, it must be stressed, worked unconsciously on the minds of the drafters. But it has been suggested that in discussing the evolution of law[1] I have in general understated the revolutionary force of statute law, and that I conspicuously neglect the making of legislation, in which creativity, coercion, change, society, and innovation inevitably play crucial roles.[2] To this issue I want to devote the present chapter.

It should, of course, be emphasized—indeed, it can scarcely be overemphasized—that of the forms of lawmaking that have been used in the Western world—namely custom, judicial precedent, juristic opinion, and legislation—the last is by its nature the one least bound to the legal tradition. In Chapter 4, I will claim that jurists and judges can be and frequently are opportunistic in lawmaking but, when they are, some justification, express or implied, inside the legal system is required. The judge in a customary law system can decide that a custom exists when it does not, inventing it or adopting it from elsewhere, and in the act of so doing he provides the best future evidence for the existence of the custom. But that judge can only invent within the confines of the case and moreover he must give plausibility to the decision. The judge in a system that gives binding force to precedent can again be inventive, but that innovation is restricted to the facts of the case and the judge must again operate sufficiently within the system to make his reasoning and decision plausible. Jurists in their writings can be far more inventive and can also range over a whole topic, but their views have legal effect only when they are taken over authoritatively into the system. In any event, as I have tried to show elsewhere, customary law, judicial precedent, and juristic interpretation are all made within the context of a particular legal tradition. The authors of the law do not escape from the tradition and the culture of the legal elite to which they belong.[3]

Legislation is different. It can break entirely with the existing tradition and even, in theory, with any legal tradition. It can remake the whole of a legal system. It can be the work of parliamentarians, dictators, or kings who need have no knowledge of, or no respect for, the legal tradition. This I have already indicated elsewhere.[4] Moreover, it is obvious. Creativity can exist, as indeed can coercion. Legislation can also best be used to direct the society along particular economic, religious, or political lines. Society or sections of it can bring greater pressure for change on legislation than on other means of lawmaking. All this is beyond question. The issue I would like to discuss in this chapter is rather different. To what extent in practice is legislation innovative and free from the existing legal tradition, revolutionary in law, actively used to pursue social goals, and effectively creative for society? Obviously there is no one answer, valid for every time and place. My aim therefore is more limited, to show from the lessons of Western legal history that forces habitually have operated to restrict the creativity of legislation and to inhibit it from directing society along specific and detailed lines desired by the political elite.

Again, I can only work from specific examples, but I hope to give sufficient of these to show that they do permit a considerable degree of generalization. Some of these I have used before, but their repetition here is no sign of a lack of other examples. The value of particular examples lies in their probative force, not in their novelty. Further, I am not concerned with public, including constitutional, law, because that is not my area of competence, but only with private, commercial, and criminal law. I will produce various propositions supported by examples, but the propositions shade into one another.

The first proposition is that at least until recent times, legislation has played a very restricted role in developing private, commercial, and criminal law. The main examples will be chosen from ancient Rome, with concentration on the late Republic, when lawmaking was most innovative, since that is probably the most progressive secular legal system the world has known. Examples will also be drawn from English law in the eighteenth and most of the nineteenth century, since English law, too, is highly regarded for its originality.

The last two centuries of the Roman Republic, until Octavius (later to be Augustus) was given tribunician power *in perpetuum* in 36 B.C., seem to have produced the greatest advances[5] in private law that the world has known. But what role did statute law play in this? If we begin earlier and rather arbitrarily at 300 B.C., we can take account of the *lex Aquilia*, whose final formulation is traditionally dated around 287 B.C.[6] This, the most important of all Roman statutes on private law—with the exception of the early codification, the XII Tables—is in three chapters. Chapter 1 deals with the killing of slaves and four-footed herd animals, Chapter 2 with a small technical point of contract law, and Chapter 3 (at least eventually, since its original scope is disputed) with the wounding of slaves and four-footed herd animals, the killing or wounding of other animate property, and damage to all kinds of inanimate property.

There were various statutes covering personal guarantors, and they should be taken together. By the *lex Furia*, of perhaps around 200 B.C., which applied only to Italy, the *sponsor* and *fidepromissor* (two kinds of guarantors) were relieved of liability after two years and each was liable only for an aliquot share. The earlier *lex Appuleia* introduced a kind of partnership between *sponsores* and *fidepromissores*, and anyone who paid more than his share could recover from the others. The *lex Cicereia*, whose date cannot be established, declared that anyone about to take *sponsores* or *fidepromissores* had to give prior notice and declare both the matter and the number of guarantors. The *lex Cornelia*, of around 81 B.C., forbade the same person to be guarantor for the same debtor in the same year for more than 20,000 sesterces of loaned money.[7]

The *lex Cincia* of 204 B.C. forbade gifts in return for defense in court and gifts in general above a certain (unknown) amount to anyone outside a specified relationship. Very shortly thereafter came the *lex Plaetoria* (or *Laetoria*), which gave an action against one who defrauded a minor and a defense to the minor if he were sued on the transaction.[8] The *lex Atilia* of uncertain date, but 210 is usually thought likeliest, allowed at Rome the praetor and a majority of the tribunes of the plebs to appoint a *tutor* to a person who had none.[9] The *lex Titia* of around 99 B.C. extended similar powers to magistrates in the provinces.

There were four statutes concerning testate succession. The *lex Furia testamentaria* of somewhere between 204 and 169 B.C. enacted that no one, apart from certain classes of persons, could take more than 1,000 *asses* by way of legacy. The *lex Voconia* of 169 B.C. declared that a person classed in the first class of citizens in the latest census could not appoint a woman as heir, and that no one could take, by legacy or *mortis causa* gift, more than the heirs took. The *lex Falcidia* of 40 B.C. enacted that a testator could not leave more than three-quarters of his estate in legacies.[10] The *lex Cornelia*, probably of 81 B.C., confirmed the validity of testaments made by those who, captured by the enemy, died in captivity.

The *lex Atinia* of the first half of the last century B.C. prohibited prescription of stolen property until it had first been returned to its owner. The *lex Minicia* of before 90 B.C. declared that children born of parents who did not have the right of civil law marriage took the lowest status. The *lex Scribonia* of around 50 B.C. prevented the prescription of servitudes.

These constitute all the statutes on private law at the time when Roman law was most inventive. Other governmental devices introduced contracts such as sale, hire, mandate, and the modern form of partnership; good faith came to play an important role in legal thought; and a very great deal of the law of succession was made afresh by the edict of the praetor.[11] The only statute of outstanding importance from the period, even for the Romans, was the *lex Aquilia;* some of the others, as we have seen, appear in groups, on guarantors or on testate succession.[12] Yet legislation on public law or on political matters was abundant. There are sixteen known statutes on private law, at least 502 on political, criminal, or procedural matters.[13] The great majority of the latter are concerned with transient, particular issues—these cannot wait, but the broad eternal issues of private law can. The disproportion between private law and other legislation for this period can stand as an example—not extreme— of the typical interests of legislatures.

English law until nearing the end of the nineteenth century tells the same story: a paucity of general statutes covering what we would term private law or mercantile law. W. R. Cornish expressly observes that the statutes that in the mid-nineteenth century "introduced divorce by judicial act, incorporation with limited liability by simple registration, and patents for inventions without elaborate formalities were all more concerned with procedural machinery than with substantive doctrine."[14] A glance at the relevant portion of the *Chronological Table of the Statutes,* which gives a list of the acts of the parliaments of England, Great Britain, and the United Kingdom,[15] will show the extent to which the parliaments devoted their time much more to issues of local importance, taxation, and matters of temporary significance.

It will be enough here to take a slice in time, chosen at random, covering in this instance the first six years of the reign of George III, 1760–1766. During this period, there were 493 acts of the realm, of which only three, Infant trustees and mortgages Act, 1763 (4 Geo 3) c.16; Insolvent debtors relief Act, 1765 (5 Geo 3) c.41; and Unfunded debt Act, 1766 (6 Geo 3) c.15, would seem by the title accorded to them in the *Chronological Table* to be general statutes covering private law. But the first of these simply extended the provisions of an act of the seventh year of Queen Anne to infants with land situated within the Duchy of Lancaster, the counties palatine of Chester, Lancaster, and Durham, and the principality of Wales. The second basically was concerned with procedural or administrative matters: gaolers of prisoners for debt had to make lists of prisoners for debt and give an oath concerning the accuracy of the lists in prescribed forms; schedules of the prisoners' estates had to be made, and so on. The third in fact is officially entitled "An act for raising a certain sum of money by loans or exchequer bills, for the service of the year one thousand seven hundred and sixty six." The general tenor of statutes of the period can be illustrated by the subjects of a few from 1760: civil list (c.1); taxation (cc.2,3); South Sea Company (c.5); marine mutiny (c.8); grants to George Keith (c.15); Cornwall roads (c.32). A similar picture emerges if we choose other slices of time even from the later reign of William IV and from most of Victoria's. Indeed, Bernard Rudden expressly observes that from the Abolition of Tenures Act of 1660, "Parliament did not thereafter intervene substantially in private law until well into the nineteenth century."[16]

For continental Europe up to the time of the great codifications, the story is likewise of little legislation for private law. A short cut can be taken to demonstrate this. From the eleventh century onward, the great development factor was the Reception of Roman Law. The extent of the Reception varied from place to place. But however much one wants to restrict the extent of the Reception it nonetheless occurred, as all will agree, on a massive scale. This could not have happened if the developing private law was much changed in each individual state by legislation[17]—unless, of course, it was legislation that introduced Roman law into the particular locality!

I am not suggesting that the legislative assemblies of Republican Rome (the *comitia centuriata* and, more particularly for private law, the *concilium plebis*) were akin in constitution and outlook to the United Kingdom's Parliament in the eighteenth and nineteenth centuries—or that these were very similar to the legislators or legislative bodies in Europe from the eleventh to the eighteenth centuries. My first point is that in general they—and other legislatures too—shared a common feature: they did not give high priority to legislating on private law. The same outlook will be seen in certain other propositions.

The second proposition is that once legislation is in place it is often very difficult to dismantle or replace it. Yet if one claims that legislation can be revolutionary, adapted to the particular circumstances of the moment, then it follows that the legislation is revolutionary and makes a great leap only at the time of promulgation. If it remains in force for centuries, when societal conditions have changed, then it is, if anything, a hindrance to social efficiency. Certainly, the legislation will come to be interpreted in different ways by later courts, but then all the factors that operate to blind legal decisions will be in operation. In the first chapter, we saw one massive example of the long life of a statute in arts. 1382 through 1386, under changing social conditions of the French *code civil*, though these provisions were scarcely revolutionary—but little legislation is. Here the examples will be the two best-known pieces of legislation from the Roman Republic: the XII Tables, the code of the mid-fifth-century B.C., and the *lex Aquilia* on damage to property in the third century B.C. From English land law, we will examine one item, the Statute of Uses; for post-Roman continental Europe and the New World, we will discuss, respectively, the *Visigothic Code* and the *Ordenaçoes Filipinas*.

The traditional date of the XII Tables is around 451 B.C., and no better dating has yet surfaced.[18] The compilation was in no sense akin to modern codes; there was no attempt at completeness, and there had to be a specific reason for the inclusion of a particular provision—whether this was because the provision represented an innovation or confirmed an existing practice as law or for some other reason. In any event, because of their nature, the XII Tables could not or should not have represented a barrier to subsequent law creation. But the codification was never abolished, though some provisions were replaced by statute. This seems to have occurred as early as 445 B.C., when, by the *lex Canuleia*, the prohibition of intermarriage between patricians and plebeians, which had been introduced by the XII Tables,[19] was abolished. Again, the *lex Aquilia* seems, in the third chapter, which is presumably the latest (and hence closest to the traditional date of 287 B.C. for the complete statute), to have been primarily intended to provide a more flexible measurement of damages for injuries to slaves than was permitted by the XII Tables.[20] Likewise, praetorian edicts modified the scope of the XII Tables. This was the case with the *edictum generale* on *iniuria*, which, by substituting flexible damages for *membrum ruptum, os fractum*, and *iniuria* (all of which were types of assault on

41

the body), in effect destroyed their individuality and, whatever the intention may have been, created a new law of personal injuries, particularly where the victim was free. This was also true of the edicts on succession, and of various other edicts.[21] The edicts could not abolish the rules of the XII Tables, but they would supersede them in practice.

The jurists, as the interpreters of law, had to deal with the XII Tables, and if we look at the later Republic we will find a curious picture. In only six surviving texts do jurists refer expressly to the XII Tables, and only one of those texts concerns interpretation. But when we look more widely at cases involving extreme interpretations we find quite a number of texts relating to the interpretation of the XII Tables, but that code is never specifically mentioned. The explanation can only be that the code was relevant and important but seen as old-fashioned. Its reputation was enormous,[22] hence the fact that it was often unsatisfactory for modern use caused embarrassment. Therefore, although it had to be interpreted very freely, the jurists preferred not to say what they were doing to it.[23]

There may have been psychological reasons for not repealing the XII Tables, but these cannot apply to the survival of the most famous individual Roman statute, the *lex Aquilia*. Whatever the legislative history[24] and the original scope of the statute,[25] difficulties in practice and theory soon emerged and continued for centuries, because the *lex Aquilia* was never repealed.

Thus, we can dispose quickly of Chapter 2. It gave an action against an *adstipulator*, a subsidiary creditor, who, depending on one's interpretation of the sole informative text, *G.*3.215, either released the debtor by a mechanism known as *acceptilatio* without receiving payment or received payment and released the debtor but did not hand over the sum to the true creditor.[26] Gaius tells us in the succeeding text that the chapter was unnecessary since the action on mandate would meet the case, except that the action under the *lex Aquilia* was for double damages against a defendant who denied liability. Gaius is historically inaccurate since the *actio mandati* came into being long after the enactment of the *lex Aquilia*, but what he says might seem to suggest that the action on the *lex Aquilia* was already obsolete,[27] as it certainly was by the time of Justinian.[28]

But the main problems with the aging and reinterpretation of the statute concern Chapters 1 and 3. Chapter 1 gave an action for kill-ing (for which the verb *occidere* was used) a slave or four-footed herd animal. For some reason the verb *occidere* came to be interpreted narrowly and was restricted to cases of direct physical contact be-tween the body of the victim and the body of the wrongdoer. This interpretation was unnecessary and is not to be found elsewhere, for instance in connection with the *lex Cornelia de sicariis et venefi-ciis*, which dealt with murder. Other wrongful deaths for the pur-poses of the *lex Aquilia* were cases of "furnishing a cause of death," *mortis causam praestare,* and gave rise not to an action on the stat-ute but rather to an *ad hoc* praetorian remedy. For example, if one person by pushing another caused the latter to kill some slave, the latter was not liable because he was not at fault, nor was the former liable under the *lex Aquilia* because he had not killed—but he was liable to an action on the facts, *actio in factum.*[29] Obviously the jurists wanted to restrict the scope of the statute as much as pos-sible—perhaps because of the doubling of damages when the de-fendant denied liability—but this approach gave rise to numerous narrow distinctions of an obviously unfortunate kind that could have been remedied by a new statute. But there was not even an edictal remedy. Chapter 3, which (at least eventually) covered the wounding of slaves and four-footed herd animals and wrongful dam-age to all other kinds of property, was similarly interpreted restric-tively. There was also a difference in the way in which the damages were assessed under the two chapters. Under Chapter 1, the dam-ages were calculated as the highest value the slave or animal had had in the past year. Under Chapter 3, the damages may have been originally the loss that appeared within thirty days, but in classical times the statute's wording was taken to mean the highest value that the slave, animal, or thing had had in the preceding thirty days.[30] The difference in the way of measuring damages may have had its origin in history, but in classical times had long outlived its usefulness. The thirty-days clause in Chapter 3 was an embarrass-ment to the jurists, and there is no surviving case that turns on it. In fact, the measure of damages seems to have been calculated as the amount of the financial loss.[31]

The *lex Aquilia* was never abolished and litigants, judges, practic-ing lawyers, and scholars had to make do with it.

From England, we need choose only one example from many

possibilities, the Statute of Uses of 1535, which, although it is well known, is particularly appropriate in the present context. In the thirteenth century, a practice had arisen in which land could be transferred to A to hold for the benefit of, or "to the use of" B, and by the fourteenth century this was a common practice. Under the common law, B had no recognized interest in the land, though the chancellors in the courts of equity were intervening to give him protection by around 1400. Thus was created in effect a duality of ownership that had considerable advantages. To begin with, the land indirectly became devisable. A's obligation to administer the land according to B's wishes did not terminate with B's death so B could direct the benefits of the equitable estate to be distributed after his death. Again, B, by assigning the use during his lifetime could evade the common law principle that conveyances should be open and notorious: for the transfer of the equitable interest all that was needed was that B's intention be clear. Further, restrictions on the creation of future interests could be avoided. Likewise, the feudal burdens which were payable on the death of the tenant could be avoided. The legal estate could be transferred to several persons acting in the capacity of A in joint tenancy and on the death of any one his share would accrue to the survivors.

Thus, to avoid the payment of the feudal duties it was enough to see to it that the estate of A never lapsed by death. The death of B was irrelevant. Moreover, the device could be used to avoid forfeiture and escheat. When a tenant committed treason, his land held by tenure at common law was forfeited to the crown, and where he was convicted or outlawed for felony, the land went to the crown for a year and a day and then escheated to his lord. Transfer of the legal estate, before the commission of the offense, with the retention of the use, could protect the financial interests of the family of one about to engage in what might be criminal conduct.

This development of the use was detrimental to the financial interests of the king, who thereby lost feudal dues. It should be noted that in general the existence of the use did not badly affect other feudal lords: what they lost in feudal dues from their vassals they gained in not paying feudal dues to their own lords. Consequently, Henry VIII sought legislation in 1529 that would have abolished uses, but this was opposed by landowners, who wished to retain the freedom to devise land, and by lawyers who profited from drafting settlements and wills. Henry responded by threatening a full inquiry into abuses of the common law, and eventually in 1535 the Statute of Uses was enacted. This statute in effect abolished the distinction between the legal and equitable estate. The statute provided that when one person was seised of lands to the use of another the latter was to have lawful seisin. Thus, B's equitable estate became the legal estate and A had no estate in the land.

Although the statute was successful in raising money for the king, it was extremely unpopular, not just because of the financial burdens it reinstated but also because it imposed of necessity primogeniture, though for some time landowners had been making their own arrangements with regard to the succession to land. As a result, the Statute of Wills was passed in 1540, permitting a tenant to devise all his socage lands and two-thirds of his lands held in knight-service. The usual decline in the value of money and the abolition in 1660 of the military tenures of feudal land-holding meant that by that date at the latest, the king had little interest in the survival of the Statute of Uses.

Nevertheless, the statute did continue to exist. Loopholes were discovered from the very beginning, but the device adopted by conveyancers that was ultimately to prevail and deprive the statute of most of its effects was to make the devise "to A and his heirs to the use of B and his heirs to the use of C and his heirs." Even before the Statute of Uses, only the use in favor of B was effective. There could not be a use upon a use. This was confirmed by cases shortly after the statute. But sometime during the seventeenth century—the steps in the process are not clear—it came to be accepted that the use to C would in fact be effective, in accordance with the testator's wishes. The statute operated to execute the first use but not the second, which for clarity was termed a "trust." In time, the accepted practice of conveyances was to omit any mention of A. The devise would be effective if it read: "unto and to the use of B and his heirs in trust for C and his heirs." The Statute of Uses was repealed in 1922 by the Law of Property Act, s.207, Schedule 7.[32]

The Statute of Uses is an instructive example in the present context. Above all, it does show—and that is the reason for its being adduced—that once a statute is in place, it is not easily removable by subsequent legislation. This is true even for private law statutes of high visibility. This remains the case even when, as here, the statute blocks a development that was regarded as desirable by those affected. It took a long time to accept as valid a devise "unto and to the use of B and his heirs in trust for C and his heirs." Yet the king's revenue from feudal dues could have been protected in other ways, as was, indeed, proposed at the time.[33] This failure of the legislature to intervene with reforming legislation remains, no matter which aspect of its history one examines: its blocking of the rational development of the trust; the disappearance of its fiscal purposes; the slow subversion of its meaning by judicial decisions; its survival solely as a trap for conveyancers. We must also notice that the Statute of Uses, however important it was in the history of English private law, was enacted primarily for fiscal purposes. Legislation, intended to affect the course of private law, was and long remained uncommon.

For longevity of legislation in continental Europe, we may refer to the *Visigothic Code* (or *Liber iudiciorum* or *Liber iudicum*) of King Recesvind, containing Visigothic laws promulgated until A.D. 654. Even after the Moorish occupation, this continued as the personal law of the *hispani* in Septimania and Catalonia. It emerged to a new importance with the reconquest, being given, in the official translation into Castilian called the *Fuero Juzgo*, which was made under Ferdinand III of Castile, to numerous towns as they were reconquered from the Moors. Subsequently, as an important part of the law of Castile, it was even exported to the New World.[34] Insofar as the *Fuero Juzgo* was displaced, it was largely replaced by the *Fuero Real* (1255) and *Las Siete Partidas*, both of Alfonso X, each of which, after a distinguished life in Spain, also crossed to the Spanish possessions in America.

Likewise, one might cite the *Ordenaçoes Filipinas*, the ordinances of Philip II of Spain, promulgated in 1603 for Portugal and hence in force also in Brazil. These ordinances were defective from the outset: obscure in language, with frequent contradictions, prolix, and above all full of gaps, especially in private law, which was the subject of book 4.[35] The many lacunae were filled principally from Roman law, which was given, along with the gloss of Accursius and the opinions of Bartolus, formal status as subsidiary law.[36] A different approach to the lacunae was taken as a result of the *Lei da Boa Razão* of 1769, which among other things forbade recourse to Accursius, Bartolus, and other doctors and declared that cases should be decided according to the spirit of the laws.[37] The *Ordenações Filipinas* remained in force when Brazil became independent in 1822 and were still the basis of private law until the promulgation of the *Codigo Civil Brasileiro* in 1917.

Milsom writes of "the nightmare results" of the Statute of Uses,[38] and he asks: "Can the draftsmen of the Statutes of Uses and of Wills reasonably be charged with lack of foresight?"[39] On one level, this seems an odd question: drafters can never be expected to foresee precisely how their legislation will come to be interpreted over a long period of time. On another level, the implication—which may not have been intended—of the question is that drafters of legislation must work under the assumption that their law will not be replaced, no matter how unsatisfactory it turns out to be. This implication, as we have seen, is accurate, and not just for England.

The third proposition (on which we need not dwell here)[40] is that there are many fields in which legislators and legislatures often seem little interested in legislating. Examples are best taken from areas of law in one country where radical change in the law is obviously needed—and known to be needed—but where none, or very little, has been forthcoming for centuries, despite a succession of legislators. This occurs both where there was once previous legislation and where there was not. The *lex Aquilia* is again an example from Rome. We can cite others. From England, we can choose the outstanding, glaring example of the failure to introduce compulsory land registration and to abolish feudal tenures, failures that existed until 1925.[41] Or, again, we might list the failure to introduce legislation to abolish the distinction between libel and slander, a distinction roundly condemned by many and supported by no academic writer of this century, or indeed the failure in general to provide the much-needed reform of the law of defamation.[42] In Scotland, the law relating to conveyancing furnishes another example.[43]

The fourth proposition is more surprising and states that even great lawmakers, famous for their legislation, have not been particularly interested in setting forth a detailed political, social, or economic message in their legislation. Although legal historians, looking at an individual code, claim to find in it very specific relations with the political and economic order, the claims often lack substance. Examples of legislators' disinterest in giving a particular message can be chosen from Justinian, through Frederick the Great and Napoleon, even to Atatürk. I am not, of course, claiming that these figures of history did not have precise political and other aims, but rather only that one cannot, at least in many contexts, find in their private law legislation a dominant concern to find the substantive law most suited for the conditions of their time. Massive legislation is itself a highly political act, but the legislators' main aim may be to clarify existing law and make it more readily available, to unify the legal rules within the state, or to modernize the law in order to help modernize the state. Such aims may fall far short of seeking the rules "most suitable" for the society.

For Justinian and his advisers one can discount, almost a priori, the notion that the substantive rules in the *Code, Digest,* and *Institutes* were in general geared to a precise societal ordering. If such had been his intention, then he would not have chosen to construct the *Code* and *Digest* on the basis of quotations of earlier law from emperors and jurists. No doubt the quotations are selective and reflect to some extent the concerns of the age, but to select statements from the past to give effect to conditions of the present is scarcely the way to set about providing legal rules precisely adapted to the contemporary world. Moreover, the *Digest,* and to a lesser extent the *Code,* reflects the pagan world of Rome, one of diverse economic conditions, not the Christian world of Constantinople. Indeed, the *Digest* and the *Code* to a considerable extent represent different worlds. Virtually no *Digest* text can be ascribed to the period after the death of Alexander Severus in A.D. 235, but by far the greater part of the *Code* belongs to the time after that date. Therefore, the former, unlike the latter, cannot reflect the economic collapse of the half-century before Diocletian, the autocracy of that and subsequent rulers, the move to Constantinople, the rise of Christianity, and the absence of independent creative jurists.

These differences between the *Digest* and the *Code* become even more significant in the present context when we recall that the two works were prepared independently of each other. The surviving evidence indicates that when Justinian ordered the preparation of the first *Code*, he did not yet have the intention of collecting, abridging, and promulgating as law the writings of the classical jurists. It is only if the *Digest* represents a second stage of his thinking about replacing the prior law that one can explain the promulgation of the *Fifty Decisions*—to settle old, yet still existing, juristic disputes—*after* the completion of the first *Code* of 529, and their subsequent incorporation into the second *Code* of 534. The *Fifty Decisions* must have been a preliminary effort to the compilation of the *Digest*. But two such different works as the *Code* and *Digest*, conceived independently under the auspices of the same emperor, belie the notion that either of them, or both together, offered substantive legal rules that as a whole contained a precise political, social, or economic message. In addition, Justinian's instructions to his compilers and the other prefaces for the first *Code*, the second *Code*, and the *Digest* contain nothing to warrant the conclusion that he wanted the excerpted texts to maintain or bring about any particular image of society. Yet we have extensive information regarding what he stated he wanted in two prefaces to the first *Code*, one setting up the commission, the other confirming the completed work; a preface confirming the second *Code*; and in two prefaces to the *Digest*, one setting up the commission for it and the other confirming it.

For Frederick the Great of Prussia it is enough to call attention to the first fruits of his attempts to codify the law, *Das Project des Corpus juris Frederici, d.h. S.M. in der Vernunft und Landes verfassungen gegründetes Landrecht, worin das Römische Recht in eine natürliche Ordnung und richtiges Systema nach denen dreyen Objectis juris gebracht*, which was published at Halle between 1749 and 1751. The very title is instructive: "The Project for the *Corpus juris Frederici*, that is, the Territorial Law of His Majesty, Founded in Reason and the Territorial Constitutions, in which Roman Law is Brought into a Natural Order and Right System in Accordance with its Three Objects of Law." That is to say, it gives the *ius commune*, and it is in fact arranged in the order of Justinian's *Institutes*. There is no attempt here to compose afresh a law peculiarly suited to the Prussian territories. Indeed, some paragraphs of the preface, particularly 15, 22, 23, and 28, make it plain that for the drafters the impetus for the *Project* was not dissatisfaction with the substantive *ius commune* but with the difficulty of ascertaining the law because of the poor arrangement of Justinian's *Corpus Juris Civilis* and of the multitude of writings by subsequent jurists. In §2 of part 1, book 1, Frederick claims it is only to be regretted that the German emperors when they received Roman law did not also systematize it. Frederick's primal intentions—at least as they were perceived by his famous chancellor, Samuel Cocceji—ought best to be revealed by the main thrust of this first production. The fact that, because of the Seven Years' War, it never came into force (which is regarded, for instance, by F. Wieacker as rather fortunate)[44] is not of consequence here. For later attempts at codification, ultimately crowned with success, with rather different aims, Frederick was indebted to a new generation of lawyers and philosophers.[45]

Indeed, even before, in the late fifteenth and sixteenth centuries, many German cities, towns, and even villages received reformed statements of their law. As Gerald Strauss has pointed out: "If one is to believe their preambles, municipal and territorial 'reformations' were undertaken in Germany for one overriding reason: to end the uncertainty affecting all areas of law by replacing the old rules with a single code combining the virtues of clarity and uniformity."[46] The main intention was not to incorporate particular political and social messages in the law, but to render intelligible the substance of the law. The fact that many "reformations" were romanizing is not in conflict with this.

Napoleon, as is continually stressed, took a strong personal interest in the preparation of the *code civil*. We have already seen in the first chapter how difficult it would be to sustain the proposition that the provisions give a substantive law geared toward a particular political, social, or economic message. None at least can be found in the bases of liability for delict. The same is true in other fields. This time we should examine a branch of the law in which customary law predominated and in which we should expect to find the impact of new ideas. What effect, one might wonder, did revolutionary and Napoleonic fervor have on the law of matrimonial property? And what growth of awareness is shown by the legislative history?

Art. 1387 of the *code civil* declares that the law does not regulate the conjugal association with regard to property except in the absence of special agreements that spouses can make as they judge fit, provided they are not contrary to good morals. This freedom to con-

tract is not ancient. Until the sixteenth century, the choice of matrimonial regime was unknown. Only one regime operated in each
region of France: in the *pays de droit coutumier* this was community of property, and the precise arrangements varied from place to
place; in the *pays de droit écrit* and also in Normandy, this was a
system of dowry.[47] Art. 1390 forbids spouses to stipulate in a general
manner that their association will be regulated by one of the customs or other law that previously governed the different parts of
French soil and that were abolished by the *code*. Art. 1391 states
that the parties could declare in a general manner that they were
marrying under the regime of community of property or under the
dotal regime. In the first alternative, the arrangement was said to be
governed by arts. 1399 to 1539 of the *code* (though actually it was
governed by arts. 1399 to 1496, the first part of the second chapter),
and in the second alternative by arts. 1540 to 1581 of the *code*. Art.
1393 enacts that, in the absence of special arrangements for the
property of the spouses, arts. 1399 to 1496 formed the common law
of France.

Thus by the *code civil* of 1804, spouses could make their own
arrangements governing their property, but if they failed to do so,
the marriage was with community of property under the particular
regime described and enacted in arts. 1399 to 1496. That same regime also applied if the spouses declared in a general manner that
they were married with community. In terms of their freedom to
make their own arrangements, the spouses could also agree that the
wife would bring the husband a dowry. If they declared in a general
manner that the marriage would have a dotal regime, then the parties' rights were governed by arts. 1540 to 1581.

What, therefore, is this one regime of community property that
was declared to be the common law of France, and this one dotal
regime that applied when a dotal regime was declared but not further specified? How did the *code* drafters come up with these rules,
and what are the origins of the rules?

Of the various community regimes—and there were approxi-
mately sixty—at the time of the French Revolution, that of the
Coutume de Paris was by far the most widespread and could even
be described as the common law of France. It was the provisions of
this *Coutume* that in very large measure formed the basis of the

provisions on the *communauté légale*. There seems to have been little determined search for other, better, or newer rules. The discussions in the Conseil d'Etat in September and October 1803 are instructive.[48] Apart from the preliminary issue of whether there should be a common law, there was relatively little discussion or disagreement about the substance of the provisions. By far the most lively argument was provided by Maleville in his unsuccessful opposition to what became art. 1401. It is his arguments and those of Berlier, who opposed him, that are significant. Maleville objected that by that provision, successions and gifts of movables to one spouse would be shared with the other. He argued:

> This principle is so extraordinary that even in the *coutumes* which accept community, it is usual to stipulate that spouses will not be liable for each other's debts; that their movables will remain their own in whole or in part; that the same will apply to successions or gifts that may come to them; that in out of one hundred contracts of marriage made even in Paris, there is not ten where one is held to the statutory community as it is presented here. And one would like to give it as a rule to those who have always rejected it![49]

And the beginning of Berlier's response was:

> In reducing the conjugal community of property to a simple partnership of acquisitions, M. Maleville proposes to derogate from the most general practices of the *pays de droit coutumier:* for the *coutume* of Paris, whose ressort was immense, and the majority of the others, brought together into the community the respective movables of the spouses. And that consideration has already some weight, for one must not innovate without serious reasons.[50]

Thus, Maleville was opposed to one provision in the *code civil* that followed the *Coutume de Paris* on the precise ground that even in Paris the rules in it were not wanted and that, of those who made marriage contracts, more than 90 percent adopted different rules. The opposing argument, which was successful, was precisely that the provision did give the rules of the *Coutume de Paris* and of the *coutumes* in general, and that one should not innovate without strong reason. Nothing is more powerful than these arguments for demonstrating the absence of revolutionary zeal in reforming the law of marital property.

The rules for the dotal regime in arts. 1540 to 1581 are equally significant in the failure of the *code* to give a particular new political, social, or economic message, since in general they simply give the rules of Roman law as they had come to be understood in the *pays de droit écrit.* Indeed, art. 1559 introduced Roman law that had not previously been received: according to Duveyrier, when the project was communicated to the *tribunat* this was because the reasons for the Roman rule were foreign under the ancien régime but the new political institutions were like those of the Romans.[51] And it can scarcely be emphasized too much that the proposed rules on dowry had given rise to little debate in the Conseil d'Etat.

But we must go slightly further back. The *projet* for a code that the commission presented on 24 thermidor, an VIII, dealt only with the rules of community property, statutory and by special agreement, and were silent on dowry. This caused such a furor in the Midi that the later *projet* contained numerous provisions on dowry.[52] Thus was confirmed the prophecy of Estienne Pasquier (1529–1615): "Ask those who are nourished in the *pays de droit écrit,* they will tell you that separation of property is, beyond compare, better than community, and those of the *pays de droit coutumier* will give their judgment in favor of community of property. So much tyranny has a long and ancient usage over us."[53]

The nature of the point I am making about the *code civil* should perhaps be spelled out. In no sense am I claiming that the French Revolution and subsequent events had no impact upon French private law. Of course they did, notably with regard to personal status and the abolition of feudal notions of property. Rather I am insisting that in the many fields in which there was no obvious, immediate, revolutionary promulgation, the drafters of the code, despite all their debates, gave rules that were rooted in the past, in the purely legal tradition at that, and that cannot be explained on the basis of some particular, political, social, economic, or moral message. It can in no way surprise us that legal change, indeed even drastic change, can be promulgated by statute: the surprising thing, to my mind, is the extent to which change does not occur.

Over Atatürk there is no need to linger, since I have recently outlined elsewhere his law reform.[54] Atatürk, who wished to reform and modernize Turkish life in so many ways (and was very largely successful), had promulgated in 1926 the Turkish civil code (*Türk Kanunu Medenîsi*), which contained virtually all of the two Swiss codes, the *Schweizerisches Gesetzbuch* and the *Obligationenrecht*. Substantive alterations were few and minor. But what is striking is that the two Swiss codes were regarded by their creators as particularly Swiss and in accordance with the Swiss national spirit and moral consciousness. Yet, writing in the context of Turkish marriage law, N. Y. Gürpinar can claim: "In addition, after the revolution in Turkey it was urgently necessary to create a law corresponding to the principles of the young Turkish republic. This for civil law was the Turkish civil code taken over from Switzerland."[55] And in a more general context, after explaining the need for a modern Turkish code, B. N. Esen writes:

> That was the situation of fact. Now, Switzerland always was and is the land of democracy *par excellence*. As a land with a long democratic past Switzerland was quite especially called to serve as a model for the civil code. Turkey did not hesitate a single second. And in 1926 were the *Schweizerisches Gesetzbuch* and the Swiss *Obligationenrecht* taken over with minor alterations as the statute law of the state. If these codes of foreign origin have been used in Turkey for a quarter century without the slightest difficulty, then it is on this account, because they mirror exactly the spiritual inclination of the social milieu, that they reflect the idea of law and justice of the place in which they are interpreted and used.[56]

Thus, so far as private and commercial law are concerned, a revolutionary leader seeking democracy in Turkey could find almost precisely what he needed in codes framed for very different conditions in Switzerland.

Perhaps even more surprising is the extent to which private law in the Soviet Union remains true to its nonsocialist past. There is a debate among theorists as to whether Soviet law should be classed among civil law systems or as a separate family.[57] But it is common ground that German law, especially in the form of *Pandektenrecht*, was of great significance for Russian law before the Revolution, as indeed can easily be seen in draft codes. This influence in fact continues, as appears from the structure of the civil code of the Russian

Soviet Federative Socialist Republic (RSFSR) of 1964. Thus, part 1, "General Principles," corresponds closely to the first book, the *Allgemeiner Teil*, of the German *BGB*, even including the same subject matter (and classifications), such as legal transactions, calculation of time, and limitation of actions by the passage of time—and omitting the same subjects, such as things. Part 2 contains the law of property and part 3 the law of obligations, whereas the *BGB* deals with obligations in book 2 and the law of things in book 3.

But it is precisely here that the Russian code follows the developed system of *Pandektenrecht* as set out, for instance, by B. Windscheid in *Lehrbuch des Pandektenrechts*[58] and which was inverted in the *BGB*. The Russian civil code of 1922 contained as its fourth and final book—part 7 in the 1964 code—the law of succession, which corresponds exactly to the fifth and final book of the *BGB*. The 1964 code, unlike that of 1922, contains books that have no counterpart in the *BGB*, on copyright, the right to discoveries, the law of inventions, and the legal capacities of aliens and stateless persons, but these in turn reflect a trend in Western civil law systems to include such subjects in modern civil codes.

More interesting than the survival of the Pandectist structure in the RSFSR civil code is the survival of presocialist law. Almost all of the articles of the code owe their substance and formulation to pre-existing Pandectist or customary rules. Indeed, only ten articles or parts of ten articles can be designated as socialist rather than as rooted in the preceding legal tradition: arts. 1(1); 5; 93; 96(3); 105(3); 106; 107; 111; 137(2); and 434.[59]

Again, the point I am making must be stressed. I am not claiming that all of private law is free from politics or that politics does not have a great impact on law. The law contained in the ten provisions just mentioned of the RSFSR civil code does give profound changes. The point rather is that so much of the old law that is of practical significance remains, not because of any particular message, but simply because it is there. In this context, Martin Krygier correctly claims that in all traditions, a transmitted past (real or believed to be real) is treated by participants as an authoritatively significant part of their present.[60]

The final proposition is that revolutionary proposals for law reform, even in a time of revolution, are often rejected by legislatures, or are watered down to lose much of their message. Examples here are the draft codes of Cambacérès in France, and Jeremy Bentham's unsuccessful attempts to persuade governments to look seriously at his proposals for codification.

At the time of the French Revolution, France was a state in which different localities each had their own legal system. As early as 5 July 1790, the Assemblée Nationale Constituante decreed that the "civil laws would be reviewed and reformed by the legislators, and that a general code of simple laws, clear and fitted (*appropriées*) to the constitution will be made." And this was confirmed in the 1791 constitution: "There will be made a code of civil laws, common to the whole kingdom." The Convention Nationale decreed on the 25 June 1792 that its legislative committee should be bound to produce within one month a *projet* of the civil code. Cambacérès' completed first *projet* was announced to the convention on 7 August 1792.[61]

When contrasted with preceding law, this short first *projet* was revolutionary in character. Thus, for example, from the law of persons, *titre* III, art. II introduced an equal right of administration by husband and wife of their common matrimonial property. *Titre* IV, art. 5 in effect abolished the status of bastard, declaring that a person who did not know his or her parents was to be termed an orphan. *Titre* V, art. 2 declared that the principal duty of parents, after nourishing and raising their children, was to teach or have them taught a trade in agriculture or of a mechanical type; the penalty for failure being to provide them with aliment their whole lives long. *Titre* VI regulated divorce, and provided for it a simple mechanism before, and by decision of, a family council; no grounds were needed for divorce, and no penalties were imposed on a spouse who misbehaved. Adoption—just recently accepted in France—was regulated in *titre* VII; anyone over the age of majority, whether single or married, could adopt, a married couple could adopt in common, and adoption by one spouse required the consent of the other.

Cambacérès himself set out his intentions. He wanted

> to raise the great edifice of civil legislation; an edifice simple in its structure, but majestic in its proportions; great in its very simplicity, and so much the more solid that, not being built on the moving sands

of systems, it will rise on the firm soil of the laws of nature, and on the virgin earth of the Republic.[62]

Again, "The legislator must not aspire to say everything: but, after having set out fecund principles that in advance set aside many doubts, he must seize on developments that leave few questions remaining."[63]

After much debate, this first *projet* was in effect abandoned as being too complicated—that is not how it appears to a modern reader!—and Cambacérès produced a second *projet*, which he presented at the Convention Nationale on 9 September 1794. This was at once regarded as having the opposite faults—too concise and philosophical—and a committee of seven was set up to organize a code. Soon the committee was enlarged to eleven and Cambacérès was included.[64] This resulted in Cambacérès' third *projet*, which was presented in Messidor, an IV, and on this occasion he said:

> Now that everything today has been changed in the political order, it is necessary to substitute for the old laws a code of simple laws, whose redaction aids understanding, and which are, at the same time, the principle of social happiness and the safeguard of public morale.
>
> It is in this spirit that the first *projet* of the civil code was drafted. In discussing it, the Convention Nationale soon uncovered various flaws, the inevitable result of the speed with which the work had been conceived and executed. To make them disappear the legislative committee gave particular importance to separating principles from implications, rules from corollaries, and to reducing the work to a collection of precepts where each one could find the rules for his conduct in social life. Whatever advantage this method could produce, it could not satisfy the impatience of the nation or the views of the legislative body. Where judges are not legislators, it does not suffice to ensure the authority of laws by justice; it is also necessary that they are so set out as to remove doubt by clarity, to foresee exceptions by foresight. Thus, without aspiring to say everything, the legislator must lay down fecund principles which can in advance resolve many doubts, and take hold of developments which will leave few questions remaining. Such are the views which guided the commission for classifying laws in the *projet* of the code which it presents to you.[65]

This third *projet* was likewise doomed. Despite valiant attempts at codification and despite three awe-inspiring *projets*, the age of revolution was not to create a revolutionary code of law in France.

In this context it is instructive also to look at Jeremy Bentham's unsuccessful attempts to persuade governments to look seriously at his proposals to provide model codes. He wrote in such terms to the president of the United States of America,[66] to the governor of Pennsylvania,[67] in a circular to the governors of the American United States,[68] and to the emperor of all the Russias.[69] The significant point is not so much that his proposed codes never became legislation but that, on receipt of his offers to produce codes, no political leader asked him to provide a draft. That his codes would have been radical there is no doubt. In his letter of May 1814 to the emperor of all the Russias he wrote:

> SIRE,—the object of this address is to submit to your Imperial Majesty an offer relative to the department of legislation.
> My years are sixty-six. Without commission from any government, not much fewer than fifty of them have been occupied in that field. My ambition is to employ the remainder of them, as far as can be done in this country, in labouring towards the improvement of the state of that branch of government in your Majesty's vast empire.
> In the year 1802, a work, extracted, as therein mentioned, from my papers, was by *Mr. Dumont of Geneva*, published at Paris, in three volumes, 8[vo.] under the *title of Traités de Législation Civile et Pénale*, &c.
> In the year 1805, a translation of it into the Russian language was published at St. Petersburg, by order (if I am rightly informed) of your Majesty's government.
> Since the publication of that work, Europe has seen *two* extensive bodies of law promulgated within its limits: one by the *French Emperor*, the other by *the King of Bavaria*. These two are the only bodies of law of any such considerable extent, that have made their appearance *within the last half century*. Of the one promulgated by the *French Emperor*, a complete *penal* code formed a part. In the preface to that authoritative work, my un-authoritative one is mentioned with honour: among the *dead, Montesquieu, Beccaria,* and *Blackstone;* among *living* names, (unless it be for some *matter of fact*) none but *mine*. In the Bavarian code, drawn up by *Mr. Bexon*, much more *particular as well as copious mention* is made of that work of mine, much more *eulogy* bestowed upon it.
> In *France*, under the immediate rod of Napoleon—in *Bavaria*, under the influence of Napoleon—the generosity displayed by the notice thus taken of the work of a living Englishman, could not but call forth my admiration.
> Approbation is one thing; adoption is another. With mine before

them, both these modern works took for their basis the jurisprudence of ancient Rome. Russia, at any rate, needs not any such incumbrance. . . .

Codes upon the *French* pattern are already in full view. Speak the word, Sire, *Russia* shall produce a pattern of her own; and then let Europe judge.

"Approbation" but not "adoption" could serve as the epitaph of most attempts at reform of the law through legislation.

Thus, though legislation can be the most radical mode of changing law, and though it does at times make radical, even revolutionary, changes in law, its history in the Western world is largely one of a failure to make anything approaching the use of its potential.

NOTES TO CHAPTER 2

1. Watson, *Evolution*.

2. A. London Fell, *American Historical Review* 91 (1986): 85.

3. Watson, *Evolution*.

4. See, e.g., Watson, "Legal Change," especially at pp. 1156f.; also see Watson, *Sources of Law*, pp 11f.

5. "Advances" is, of course, an ambiguous term. I do not think a precise explanation need be proffered, but I am thinking of changes in the law that had a long-term impact.

6. See e.g., Rotondi, *Leges*, p. 241. But A. M. Honoré, for instance, prefers a date between, say, 209 and 195 B.C. See "Linguistic and Social Context of the *lex Aquilia*," *Irish Jurist* 7 (1972): pp. 138ff., especially at p. 149.

7. On all of these, see *G.*3.118–125.

8. See, e.g., Rotondi, *Leges*, pp. 271f.

9. See, e.g., Kaser, *Privatrecht*, 1, p. 357.

10. For details, see, e.g., A. Watson, *The Law of Succession in the Later Roman Republic* (Oxford: Clarendon Press, 1971), pp. 163ff.

11. The higher Roman elected public officials had the right to issue edicts setting out how they saw their tasks. Those magistrates in charge of the courts, notably the praetors and *curule aediles*, issued edicts setting out the circumstances in which they would grant an action. Thus, though they did not technically have lawmaking powers, they had an enormous impact on legal change.

12. We need not consider which assemblies were responsible for private law legislation.

13. See the statutes collected in Rotondi, *Leges.*

14. In Coing, *Handbuch*, 3, p. 2218.

15. *Part 1* (London, H.M.S.O., 1981), pp. 9ff.

16. "Comparative Law in England" in *Comparative Law and Legal System*, ed. W. E. Butler and V. N. Kudriavtsev (New York: Oceana, 1985), pp. 79ff.

17. But against the idea that there was no medieval legislation, see A. Wolf, "Gesetzgebung and Kodifikation," in *Die Renaissance der Wissenschaften im 12. Jahrhundert*, ed. P. Weimar (Zurich: Artemis, 1981), pp. 143ff.

18. See, e.g., Watson, *Transplants*, pp. 13ff. and the references given.

19. See, e.g., Watson, *XII Tables*, pp. 20ff.

20. See the provisions habitually numbered 8.2,3,4.

21. For details, see Watson, *Law Making*, p. 112.

22. See, e.g., Cicero, *de oratore*, 1.44.195.

23. For the argument, see Watson, *Law Making*, pp. 112ff.

24. The very different Chapter 2 sandwiched between Chapters 1 and 3 suggests that there were at least two stages, with Chapter 3 an addition to the existing Chapters 1 and 2, probably around 287 B.C. See, above all, D. Daube, "On the Third Chapter of the *Lex Aquilia*," *Law Quarterly Review* 52 (1936): 253ff. at 268.

25. The original scope and meaning of Chapter 3 have been much disputed; see, e.g., Kaser, *Privatrecht*, 1, p. 161, and the references he gives.

26. See, above all, H. Lévy-Bruhl, "Le Deuxième Chapitre de la loi Aquilia," *Revue Internationale des Droits de l'Antiquité* 5 (1958): 507ff.

27. See, e.g., F. De Zulueta, *The Institutes of Gaius*, 2 (Oxford: Clarendon Press, 1953), p. 216.

28. *J.*4.3.12.

29. *D.*9.2.7.3. See also *infra*, Chapter 3.

30. *G.*3.218. The text betrays the difficulties of the jurists in giving a meaning to the wording of the *lex.*

31. This emerges clearly from *D.*9.2.24. This appears as a coda to the preceding 23.11; hence it cannot be interpolated in substance. (It contains something that was not in *h.t.*23.11 of Ulpian but was found by the compilers or their forerunners in Paul, and they added it. If the text were the work of the compilers, they would simply have inserted it in the midst of the quotation from Ulpian.) It is in the form of a rhetorical question; hence, the expected answer is assumed to be the accepted opinion of the jurists. *D.*9.2.23.11 says that the *actio legis Aquiliae* will not be given if someone confesses to killing a slave who is alive. Then, in 9.2.24: "This is clearer with regard to a wounded man: for if one confessed to having wounded and he was not wounded, the estimation of what wound will we make? Or to what time will we have recourse?" The case is not clearer if damages were related to the value of the slave in the previous thirty days, but only if estimation was made of the actual injury inflicted.

32. For this abbreviated account of the Statute of Uses and its history, see, above all, E. H. Burn, *Cheshire's Modern Law of Real Property*, 12th ed. (London, Butterworths, 1976), pp. 45ff.; Baker, *Introduction*, pp. 210ff.; Milsom, *Foundations*, pp.

216ff.; A. W. B. Simpson, *History of the Land Law,* 2nd ed. (Oxford: Clarendon Press, 1980), pp. 173ff.

33. See, e.g., Baker, *Introduction,* p. 218; Milsom, *Foundations,* p. 220.

34. See, e.g., F. Tomás y Valiente, *Manual de Historia del Derecho Español,* 4th ed. (Madrid: tecnos, 1983), pp. 120ff.

35. See, e.g., Braga da Cruz, "A formação histórica do moderno direito privado português e brasileiro," *Revista da Faculdade de Direito, Universidade de São Paulo* 50 (1955): 35.

36. Book 3, title 64, preamble.

37. See, e.g., da Cruz, "A formação," pp. 62ff.: cf. L. Delgado, *Quadro Histórica do Direito Brasileiro* (Recife: Universidade Federal de Pernambuco, 1974), pp. 92ff.

38. Milsom, *Foundations,* p. 219.

39. Ibid., p. 227.

40. See, in general, A. Watson, *Society and Legal Change* (Edinburgh: Scottish Academic Press, 1977).

41. For the argument, see Watson, *Society and Legal Change,* pp. 47ff.

42. For the argument, see Watson, *Society and Legal Change,* pp. 61ff.

43. See, for example, the quotations from speeches during the passing of the Land Registration (Scotland) Act 1979 collected in the *Journal of the Law Society of Scotland* (1979), pp. 235f.

44. *Privatrechtsgeschichte der Neuzeit* (Göttingen: Vandenhoeck & Ruprecht, 1967), p. 329. The original idea of Frederick William of 1714 was even more a redaction of Roman law; see W. Wagner, "Die Wissenschaft des gemeinen römischen Rechts und das Allgemeine Landrecht für die Preussischen Staaten," in *Wissenschaft und Kodifikation des Privatrechts im 19 Jahrhundert,* ed. H. Coing and W. Wilhelm (Frankfurt am Main: Klosterman, 1974), pp. 191ff.

45. See Wieacker, *Privatrechtsgeschichte,* p. 329.

46. *Law, Resistance, and the State* (Princeton, N.J.: Princeton University Press, 1986), p. 85. See his subsequent pages for information on these reformations.

47. See L. Juliot de la Morandière, *Droit civil* 4 (Paris: Dalloz, 1959), p. 1.

48. See Fenet, *Travaux préparatoires,* 13, pp. 492ff.

49. Ce principe est si extraordinaire que, dans les coutumes même qui admettent la communauté, il est d'usage de stipuler que les époux ne seront pas tenus aux dettes l'un de l'autre; que leur mobilier leur demeurera propre en tout ou en parti; qu'il en sera de même des successions ou donations qui pourront leur advenir: en sorte que, sur cent contrats de mariage qui se passe à Paris même, il n'en est pas dix où l'on se tienne à la communauté légale telle qu'elle est ici présentée. Et l'on voudrait la donner pour règle à ceux qui l'ont toujours rejetée!

Fenet, *Travaux préparatoires,* 13, p. 550.

50. Qu'en reduisant la communauté conjugale à une simple societé d'acquêts, M. Maleville propose de déroger aux habitudes les plus générales du pays coutumier: car la coutume de Paris, dont le ressort était immense, et le plus grand nombre des autres, confondait le mobilier respectif des époux dans la communauté; et cette considération est déjà de quelque poids, car il ne faut pas innover sans de graves motifs.

Fenet, *Travaux préparatoires,* 13, pp. 551f.

51. Ibid., p. 758.

52. See, e.g., C.-B.-M. Toullier and J.-B. Duvergier, *Le Droit Civil Français*, 6th ed. 6.2 (Paris, n.d.), pp. 5ff.; 7.2, pp. 25f.

53. Intérrogez ceux qui sont soumis au pays de droit escrit, ils vous diront que la séparation de biens est sans comparaison meilleure que la communauté, et ceux du pays coutumier donneront leur arrest en faveur de la communauté de biens. Tant a de tyrannie sur nous un long et ancien usage.

Recherches de la France liv. IV. ch. XXI. To be found in his *Oeuvres* (Amsterdam, 1723), col. 411, 412.

54. "The Evolution of Law: Continued," *Law and History Review* 5 (1987): 537ff., at 550ff.

55. *Die Entwicklung des Türkischen Eherechts seit der Rezeption des Schweizerischen Zivilgesetzbuches* (Ph.D. diss. Göttingen, 1966), pp. 141f.

56. *Wie Man in der Türkei Recht Spricht* (Zurich: Scientia, 1950), pp. 16f.

57. For some references, see, e.g., Watson, *Evolution*, pp. 112ff.

58. The last edition, the ninth, dates from 1906 (Frankfurt am Main: Rütten & Loenig).

59. I owe this point to the kindness of Bernard Rudden.

60. "Law as Tradition," *Law and Philosophy* 5 (1986): 237ff.

61. See, e.g., Fenet, *Travaux préparatoires*, 1, pp. xxxvif.

62. He said:

[I]l faut élever le grand édifice de la législation civile: édifice simple dans sa structure, mais majestueux par ses proportions; grand par sa simplicité même, et d'autant plus solide que, n'étant point bâti sur le sable mouvant des systèmes, il s'élèvera sur la terre ferme des lois de la nature, et sur le sol vierge de la république.

63. "Le législateur ne doit pas aspirer à tout dire; mais, après avoir posé des principes féconds qui écartent d'avance beaucoup de doutes, il doit saisir des développemens qui laissent subsister peu de questions."

64. See, e.g., Fenet, *Travaux préparatoires*, 1, pp. viif.

65. Aujourd'hui que tout est changé dans l'ordre politique, il est indispensible de substituer aux lois anciennes un code de lois simples, dont la rélation facilite l'intelligence, et qui soient tout à la fois le principe du bonheur social et la sauf-garde de la morale publique.

C'est dans cet esprit que fut rédigé le premier projet de Code civil. En le discutant, la Convention nationale ne tarda point à découvrir en lui diverses imperfections, effet inévitable de la rapidité avec laquelle l'ouvrage avait été conçu et exécuté. Pour les faire disparaître, le comité de législation s'attacha singulièrement à séparer les principes des developpemens, les règles des corollaires, et à réduire l'ouvrage à un receuil de préceptes où chacun pût trouver les règles de sa conduite dans la vie civile. Quelque avantage que puisse présenter cette methode, elle ne saurait remplir ni l'attente de la nation, ni les vues du Corps législatif. Là où les juges ne sont point législateurs, il ne suffit pas d'assurer l'autorité des lois par la justice: il faut encore qu'elles soient disposées de manière à en écarter le doute par la clarté, à en prévenir les exceptions par la prévoyance. Ainsi, sans aspirer à tout dire, le législateur doit poser des principes féconds qui puissent d'avance résoudre beaucoup de doutes, et saisir des developments qui laissent subsister peu de questions. Telles sont les vues qui ont guidé la commission de la classification des lois dans le projet de code qu'elle vous présente.

Fenet, *Travaux préparatoires*, 1, pp. 140f.

66. *The Works of Jeremy Bentham*, 4, ed. J. Bowring (New York: Russell & Rus-

sell, 1962), p. 453. We need not here be concerned with the details of Bowring's accuracy.

67. Ibid., p. 463.
68. Ibid., p. 476.
69. Ibid., p. 514.

CHAPTER THREE

MEDICAL MALPRACTICE LAW

IN ANCIENT ROME

Marino Guarano of the University of Naples (whom we have already met in Chapter 1) says in his *Praelectiones ad Institutiones Justiniani in usum regni Neapolitani*, published in 1779, in the context of the *lex Aquilia*, which dealt with wrongful damage:

> It is a peculiarity of that statute which asserts the claim for wrongful killing, whether it was done from malice or through negligence, that even the slightest negligence (*culpa levissima*) can be brought into play in the action. A person will only be free from penalty of the law if the killing occurred by chance: *J.4.3.3; D.9.2.44pr.* Since therefore under the *lex Aquilia* a wrongful killer is held liable for even the slightest negligence, a number of situations ought to be discussed under that heading. Therefore under the *lex Aquilia* a medical doctor can be sued who, by cutting unskillfully, killed another's slave in treating him: *J.4.3.7.* For although lack of skill in a craft is itself free from negligence, a person does act negligently who publicly professes skill in it. But today lack of skill in doctors is scarcely ever called into court and to them it is permitted to kill with impunity.[1]

In eighteenth-century France, Montesquieu wrote in a chapter headed "One must not separate laws from the circumstances in which they were made":

Roman statutes declared that doctors could be punished for their negligence or for their lack of skill. In such a case they condemned to
deportation a doctor of slightly higher condition, and to death one
who was of a lower condition. By our laws it is different. The Roman
statutes were not made in the same circumstances as ours. At Rome,
whoever wished meddled with medicine; but with us, doctors are
obliged to study and to take certain degrees: they are thus thought to
know their art.[2]

Earlier, in the seventeenth century, Gerard Noodt, probably the
most celebrated of the Dutch school of elegant jurists, had written
a short treatise on the *lex Aquilia*.[3] It is a feature of Noodt's writing
that he seeks to give Roman law as it was at Rome, not as it had
come to be interpreted in subsequent ages down to his own time.
He devotes the whole of Chapter 8 to the following issue: "Whether
and how should lack of skill be counted as negligence, and what
ought to be said about weakness?" The entire chapter, with the exception of the short final paragraph on *infirmitas*, deals only with
the *imperitia* of medical doctors. His opinion, too, is that in the law
in general there was no liability for lack of skill except for matters
in which one professed knowledge.

But despite the impression created by these three writers, there
was a failure in Rome to develop any special medical malpractice
law. Indeed, even if we consider, as modern Eastern European states
do, that no distinction should be made between mental and physical
labor,[4] nonetheless the lack of emphasis on medical lack of skill or
negligence in the Roman sources seems surprising. Three issues
above all should concern us. First, why were the Roman remedies
on delict so limited? Second, why can the same be said about remedies for contract? Third, why was there no sign of a remedy for
other breaches of medical "professional" ethics, such as the breaching of a patient's confidences?[5]

But before we come to these, we must discuss the social standing
of doctors at Rome.

The ancient Roman tradition was that it was the *paterfamilias*
who treated his household, including his slaves and farm animals.[6]
Cato the elder, that upholder of Roman tradition against Greek innovation—not, of course, that he himself was not greatly influenced
by Greek culture—gives an account of a number of folk remedies,[7]

some of which involve magical rites.[8] The antiquity of the latter type appears from formulae that are gibberish: long, relentless repetition, not always clearly heard or understood, resulting ultimately with words that had no (ordinary) meaning for those using them.[9] One text of Cato, on the health of cattle, shows that for at least some vows the status of the performer, as freeman or slave, was irrelevant.[10] Within this context of the family, no law could develop, since one family member could not sue another.

Greek medicine began to come to Rome with the arrival in 219 B.C. of Archagathus from the Peloponnesus,[11] and this formed a distinct and more "scientific" tradition. In the conditions of the Roman world many of these Greek (and other) medical practitioners would be slaves or freedmen, and this in fact is reflected in the legal sources.[12] However one might divide the practitioners into "schools," however one might assess the evidence that they were or were not skilled, were or were not respected, it is undeniable that many doctors were slaves or freedmen. Although statistical evidence is not available, it is reasonable to state that the closer one gets to 219 B.C. the higher in general the proportion of slaves and freedmen among medical practitioners—apart from *patres familiarum* treating the family. We can safely assert that, where the patient was a slave and the doctor was not his master, then the likelihood is great that the doctor was either a slave or a freedman.

Even in the time of Justinian, medical practitioners could well be slaves as *C.6.43.3*, his constitution of A.D. 531, shows.[13] The opening reads:

> If the choice of a slave or other thing is left to two or three people or possibly more, or if the choice of a slave or other thing is left to one legatee, and he, dying, left several heirs, the old jurists doubted what the law should be if there was a dispute among the legatees or the heirs of the legatee, and one wished to choose a different slave or thing than the other. 1. We enact, therefore, that in all such cases the judge shall be chance; lots are to be drawn among the parties in dispute so that, whomsoever the lot favored, he has the power of choice, but he is to pay to the others the valuation of the part pertaining to them: that is to say, slaves male and female above the age of ten if they have no trade are to be valued at twenty gold pieces, if they are younger than ten they are to be counted at not more than ten gold pieces; but if they are skilled the valuation of them, whether male or female, may

go up to thirty gold pieces, except for notaries or doctors of either sex, since we wish notaries to be estimated at fifty gold pieces, doctors and midwives at sixty: eunuchs less than the age of ten are to be valued at up to thirty gold pieces, older up to fifty but, if they are craftsmen, up to seventy gold pieces.[14]

This constitution has further relevance. Not only were medical practitioners valued at three times the rate of slaves with no trade, and double the rate of skilled slaves, but they were also the most highly priced for this purpose (except for craftsmen eunuchs), and ranked even above notaries. Although medical practitioners might be slaves, when they were slaves they were generally valued more than any other kind of trained slave.

But there is another side. Some doctors were freeborn and were citizens and highly regarded. There is a Roman legal concept of *artes liberales*, services rendered by persons exercising a profession worthy of a freeman. There is no fixed list of what counted as *artes liberales*, but despite some scholarly doubts, the practice of medicine would seem to have been among them. Cicero, whose discussion is the earliest we have, wrote:

> Now as to trades and means of gaining a living, the general teaching as to which are to be regarded as gentlemanly (*liberales*) and which are vulgar is as follows. First are rejected those means of livelihood which incur people's hatred, such as tax collectors and usurers. Likewise ungentlemanly and vulgar are the livelihoods of all hired workers, whose labor, not whose artistic talent, is bought: for in their case their very wage is the reward of slavery. . . . But with regard to those professions in which either higher intelligence is required or from which society derives no small benefit, such as medicine, architecture, and the teaching of honorable matters, such are proper for those whose position in life they become. But trade, if it is on a small scale, is to be regarded as vulgar. . . .[15]

Other lists that Cicero made of the "liberal arts" are on a different level: these include philosophy, grammar, music, and mathematics;[16] or geometry, music, literature, and poetry;[17] or grammar, dialectic, rhetoric, music, and geometry;[18] but they are not concerned with "professions" such as medicine or architecture. And in 46 B.C., Cicero could write to Servius recommending in warm terms the free doctor, Asclapon, as both a friend to Cicero and a skillful medical practitioner.[19] The doctor's name indicates that he was not of Roman stock.

Seneca seems to have had an even higher regard for the superior doctor:

> I shall totally pass over those who make a benefaction mercenary because who thus gives takes account not of the person to whom he gives but on what terms, and which is directed to his own interest. Someone sells me grain: I could not live unless I bought; but I do not owe my life to him because I bought. Nor do I consider how necessary the thing was without which I could not live, but how little gratitude I owe for what I would not have had if I had not bought, in the transporting of which the merchant did not consider the size of the help to me but the gain to him. What I bought entails no obligation.
>
> "On that basis," one might say, "you would say you owe nothing to your doctor beyond his small fee, nor to your teacher, because you paid them something. But for all of these we have great affection, great respect." To that the answer is that some things are worth more than is paid for them. You buy from the doctor a thing beyond price, namely life and good health, from a teacher of the liberal arts the training of a gentleman and the cultivation of the mind. Thus to them is paid not the price of a thing but of service, because they are devoted to us, putting aside their own interests for ours. . . .
>
> My task would be endless if I sought further examples, to show that valuable things are sold for less. What then? Why do I owe more both to my doctor and my teacher nor do I discharge my obligation to them by payment? Because from doctor and teacher they pass into being a friend, and they place us under an obligation not because of their skill which they sell but by their kindly and friendly good will. . . .[20]

It would be a mistake to take this passage as indicating that Seneca would value a doctor because of his friendship rather than his skill. The significant thing is that Seneca, of the highest social rank, conceived of making a doctor his friend or, at least, of saying that a doctor was his friend. The warmth of Seneca proceeds from gratitude for the professional care, which must include the skill, of the doctor.

Congruent to the social position that might be attained by freeborn medical practitioners were the legal privileges that might be accorded them.[21] Thus, in D.27.1.6.8 (Modestinus, *book 2 of Excuses*), we read:

An extract from a rescript of Antoninus Pius, quoted in a constitution of the Emperor Commodus, shows that philosophers have immunity from tutelages. The actual words are as follows: "In all those cases, my deified father, immediately he had achieved the purple, confirmed in a constitution all existing offices and immunities, providing that philosophers, rhetoricians, grammarians, and doctors were to be immune from the function of *gymnasiarch, aedile,* chief priest, from billeting soldiers, corn buying or oil buying, nor were they to be adjudicators nor ambassadors, nor compulsorily enlisted in military service nor forced into other provincial duties, nor anything else.[22]

Other texts make it appear that the immunities were restricted to a specified small number of doctors (and others) in each city,[23] but rescripts of Constantine, such as *Codex Theodosianus (C.Th.)* 13.3.3, of A.D. 333, seem to apply more generally:

Confirming the special grants of earlier emperors, we order that doctors and professors of literature, also their wives and children, shall be free from all public duties, they shall not be subject to military service not take in quartered persons nor perform any compulsory public service, so that they may more easily train many in the liberal arts and above-mentioned studies.[24]

In another rescript, *C.Th.* 13.3.1pr., of either A.D. 321 or 324, the same emperor granted doctors freedom from being summoned to court or being subjected to other vexation under a penalty of one hundred thousand *nummi.*

It is within this very broad social context that we must discuss the development or otherwise of rules of medical malpractice law in ancient Rome. It is, I must stress, a characteristic of legal rules that they are habitually general in the sense that they apply to various different situations and various different kinds of people. For instance, marriage and divorce in law are the same in any individual state of the United States irrespective of whether the parties are Catholic or Lutheran or Hindu or Muslim. The result is that unless legal rules are divided to fit the various classes of users, the rules fail to respond adequately to needs.

We will turn first to liability in delict for a doctor's negligence or lack of skill. The earliest known Roman rules giving a remedy for physical injury were in the XII Tables, a code of around 450 B.C.

There were three provisions. One of these allowed retaliation in kind for *membrum ruptum,* if compensation could not be agreed upon. A second gave an action for 300 *asses* for *os fractum,* apparently breaking a bone, by striking with a fist or club. Slave victims were expressly covered by this provision, though the penalty when a slave was the victim—the award, of course, went to the master—was half that when the victim was free. The third provision gave an action for 25 *asses* for *iniuria,* or "wrong." The boundary lines between these three provisions are obscure and have given rise to much debate. My own explanation, which need not be insisted on here, is that *membrum ruptum* covered any injury to the body other than the most minor blows causing no real damage, and for that the penalty of 25 *asses* was laid down. A broken bone was included within *membrum ruptum* so that the *os fractum* provision overlapped with the other, but it provided a minimum penalty when a bone, of any kind, was broken as a result of a blow.[25]

Two subsequent remedies eventually came to replace these provisions of the XII Tables. Largely as a result of the devaluation of money, an edict on *iniuria* was issued in the later third century B.C. to replace the fixed penalties of the three provisions of the XII Tables. It would seem that there was otherwise no intention to change the substance of the law, but the very fact of flexible damages brought to an end any meaningful distinction here between *membrum ruptum, os fractum,* and ordinary *iniuria.*[26] The action originally required physical assault, and, whether or not this was also true of the XII Tables, it was confined to *deliberate* assault. Hence there was no fertile soil here for the growth of medical malpractice; an action for deliberate assault would seldom be appropriate. It may be mentioned in passing that the main field of operation was physical, later also verbal, assault on a free person, though assaults on slaves might also give the owner the right to an action.

The other remedy is probably older than the general edict on *iniuria.* The *lex Aquilia,* whose final version is traditionally dated to 287 B.C.,[27] gave remedies for *damnum iniuria datum,* "financial loss caused without right." The statute had three chapters. Chapter 1 gave an owner whose slave or four-footed herd animal was killed *iniuria,* "without right," an action for the highest value that the slave or animal had had in the previous year. Chapter 2 is irrelevant. Chapter 3 basically gave an owner whose slave or four-footed herd animal was wounded, or whose other animal was killed or wounded, or whose inanimate property was damaged *iniuria*, an action for the amount of loss that emerged within thirty days.[28] The original and later scope of the chapter are not entirely clear, but the wording with *si quis alteri damnum faxit, quod usserit, ruperit, fregerit iniuria*, "If anyone caused financial loss to another because he burned or damaged or broke without right," indicates that slaves were very much under consideration as the object of the wrong and that Chapter 3 replaced—again with flexible damages—the first two of our three XII Tables provisions: *ruperit* corresponds to *membrum rupit*, and *fregerit* to *os fregit*; otherwise there is no obvious point to the repetition of two terms for breaking.[29] The term *iniuria* gradually came to be interpreted as meaning primarily "maliciously or negligently."[30] For some reason that does not directly concern us (and that cannot be fully established), the statute came to be interpreted restrictively, and for an action to lie the injury had to be caused directly, "by the body to the body."[31] Thus, for Ulpian:

> Likewise if a midwife gave a drug from which the woman died, Labeo drew the distinction that if she administered it with her own hands she is regarded as having killed; but if she gave it for the woman to take herself an action on the facts ought to be given. This opinion is correct, for she rather furnished a cause of death than killed.[32]

As that very text shows, the actions on the *lex Aquilia* are obviously relevant to medical malpractice. Indeed, they are the principal remedies. But two things should be noticed that affected both Roman medical malpractice law and later perceptions of it. First, the *lex Aquilia* was not directed toward medical malpractice law specifically, but was a general remedy for loss (resulting from physical injury) wrongly caused. Second, the statute was concerned with damage to property—slaves so far as we are concerned—not with injury to free persons. In course of time, the praetor did grant an action to the *paterfamilias* when a son in his power (or other free dependent) was injured.[33] The analogy from slaves to other persons *alieni iuris* is an obvious one; but we cannot trace the development, whether through actions analogous to that of the *lex Aquilia* (whether called *actiones utiles* or *actiones in factum*) or at once directly on the *lex Aquilia.* But the implication of *D.9.2.5.3* (Ulpian, *book 18 on the Edict*)—where Julian is reported as discussing other remedies and Ulpian apparently gives an action on the *lex Aquilia*—suggests that the remedy did not exist in Julian's time; and he flourished under Hadrian and seems to have been consul in A.D. 148.[34] Other texts, too, do not give a remedy earlier than Ulpian. Eventually an *actio utilis* was given to a *paterfamilias* for physical injury to himself, though never a direct action on the *lex Aquilia,* as in *D.9.2.13* (Ulpian, *book 18 on the Edict*): "A free man has an Aquilian *actio utilis* on his own account: he has not a direct action because no one is considered to be the owner of his own limbs. . . ."[35]

We have no evidence even for the analogous action before Ulpian for injury to a free person who was *sui iuris;* we have none for the direct action even in the time of Justinian. Though they made certain exceptions, the Romans seem to have treated seriously their maxim that the body of a free man is beyond price.[36] It is perhaps not fanciful to see in this a subconscious desire to distance free persons from slaves. Considered from this perspective, even the exceptions are illuminating. Thus, by the *actio de effusis vel deiectis,* the praetor gave an action against the inhabitant when anything was poured onto a place where people commonly walked or stood: for double the value of any loss; for fifty thousand sesterces if a free man was said to have been killed; if the free man was alive and was said to have been injured for whatever seemed fair to the judge.[37] Thus, damage to property could be evaluated but not the life or health of a free man, for which respectively a fixed sum or what seemed fair to the judge was to be given. Another exception, the *actio de pauperie,* lay for damage caused by a four-footed animal:

> *D.9.1.3* (Gaius, *book 7 on the Provincial Edict*). There is now no doubt under this law that an action can be brought even on account of free persons, for instance if a quadruped injured a *paterfamilias* or a son in power. Of course, account is not taken of mutilation because a free body is not susceptible of being estimated in money, but of expenses incurred in medical treatment and of loss of employment and of employment opportunities lost because one was disabled.[38]

Unlike the *lex Aquilia,* the XII Tables' provision that established the *actio de pauperie* said nothing about the thing or person who was the object of the injury.

At any rate, the primary stress in discussions of the *lex Aquilia* will always be on actions on the statute itself, rather than on remedies modeled on these actions. Thus, when medical practitioners appeared in the texts as wrongdoers, their hapless patient (or victim) was generally a slave. And the medical practitioners then would in the general case be of the kind who treated slaves. And hence, from the argument made earlier in this chapter, the wrongdoing doctor on account of whose conduct an action was raised would have been in the general case either a slave or a freedman.

We may put the facts in the previous paragraph together. The *lex Aquilia* was the focal point for medical malpractice law in delict, but it was intended, originally and forever thereafter, as a general remedy for damage to property. In the field of medical malpractice, it primarily applied when the patient was a slave or, at best, a freedman. Since, given the Roman legal structure, there could be no action within the family, there would have been the possibility of an action only when the slave patient was treated by someone outside his household, and usually the doctor himself would have been a slave or a freedman. The force of the Roman legal tradition—of which more will be said later—was such that no similarly potent legal remedy in delict emerged once freeborn citizen patients were regularly treated by freeborn citizen doctors, and which was directed to that situation.

Within the broad context of the *lex Aquilia* (including its related ad hoc actions), which, it must be stressed, was the original and prime context for medical malpractice law, there is no sign of any idea of professional ethics enforced by law. Nor could one have expected it. The overriding responsibility of any Roman slave, even if he was a doctor, was always to his master. He was required to do as he was told without question. Indeed in a discussion of the *lex Aquilia* itself, we are told that if a slave killed at the order of his master, it was the master who was liable and the slave was not held responsible; that is to say that, on the assumption that he would be later manumitted, no civil action lay against him.[39]

The law, therefore, could not tolerate the notion—which does not even surface in discussion—that a slave doctor was entitled to keep secrets, such as patients' confidences, from his owner or could refuse to make a quick profit from dubious remedies at his owner's behest. Of course, the master was liable for a slave's wrongdoing, and if a slave fraudulently sold fake potions, even without his master's knowledge, the master would be liable in a civil action on account of any resulting injury. But, except in the most extreme cases, the law would not come between a slave and his owner.[40] It is theoretically possible to envisage the law making a master liable if a slave trained in particular skills offended against a code of ethics that was stricter than that imposed on the free population at large. But even stating such a possibility serves to uncover its unlikelihood.

The master was liable for his slave's wrongdoing under the *lex Aquilia*; in this instance, this means that the master was liable if the medical slave killed or injured another person's slave *iniuria*, intentionally or negligently, and lack of skill was equiparated to negligence:

> *J.4.3.7.* Lack of skill is also counted as negligence, for instance if a doctor killed your slave because he operated badly or gave him a harmful drug.[41]

> *D.9.2.7.8* (Ulpian, *book 18 on the Edict*): Proculus says that if a doctor operated unskillfully on a slave an action will lie either on hire or on the *lex Aquilia*.[42]

> *D.9.2.8.pr.* (Gaius, *book 7 on the Provincial Edict*): And the law is just the same if one misused a drug. But even one who operated skillfully and then neglected the aftercare will not be free from liability but is considered guilty of negligence.[43]

The mention of the contract of hire in the second of these texts proves, as we shall see, that the doctor was a slave.

Another text, *D.9.2.52.pr.* (Alfenus, *book 2 of the Digest*) tells us that if a slave died from blows, and there was no intervening cause, such as a doctor's lack of skill or the master's neglect, the assaulter would be liable for wrongful killing. But the whole topic of doctor's lack of skill seems to have been underemphasized. Nor is there any sign of that doctrine, so important in modern Western law, that a person in one of the "professions" must show a higher degree of skill than other people do in their work (or, alternatively, only for certain kinds of work is the professional held to guarantee his skill), if he is to escape liability, provided of course that he has held himself out as someone fit for the job. Indeed, the most detailed texts of all on lack of skill involve the *imperitia* of mule drivers:

> *D.9.2.8.1* (Gaius, *book 7 on the Provincial Edict*): A mule driver likewise, if through lack of skill he cannot hold in the rush of the mules, if they run down someone's slave, is commonly said to be liable on account of negligence. . . .[44]

> *D.9.2.27.34* (Ulpian, *book 18 on the Edict*): If someone entrusted his mule to a slave who was hired to drive it, and the slave tied it by its halter to his thumb, and the mule broke away with such force that it tore out the slave's thumb and rushed off, Mela writes that, if an unskilled slave was let out as experienced, an action on hire can be brought against his owner on account of breaking or disabling the mule, but if the mule was agitated by a blow or fear then the owner of the mule and of the slave have an action on the *lex Aquilia* against him who excited it. It seems to me, however, that in the case where there is an action on hire, there is also an action on the *lex Aquilia*.[45]

So far as the proposition that lack of skill equals negligence is concerned, no distinction is drawn between a doctor and a mule driver. Indeed, it is to be noted that the first of the mule driver texts is a continuation of the text *D.9.28.pr.*, which has already been quoted about doctors. Likewise, no text raises the issue that is central in modern discussion regarding how lack of skill is to be determined. A modern Western lawyer would see the situation of the mule driver and the doctor very differently. The French jurist R. Savatier writes:

> The liability of a doctor obviously cannot be judged like that of the driver of an automobile. There is a world between the two. The driver of an automobile must obey a police officer who is directing the traffic; and the rules of the Traffic Code are understandable by any lay person. The doctor, on the contrary, exercises a doubly removed profession: doubly removed through its scientific character, and by the kind of human priesthood attached to it.[46]

It is reasonable to believe that the siting of the discussion would inhibit the development of a doctor's liability in delict if he did not show special skill. To begin with, the *lex Aquilia* is general in scope, embracing the negligence of people of all kinds. There is little room here for developing the notion that lesser negligence will make some people liable but not others. At the most, there could have been the idea that what was negligence varied according to the circumstances. Again, the general approach to understanding the *lex Aquilia* would have been fixed before slaves came frequently to be given medical treatment outside the household. Notions of liability would already have been largely fixed. Furthermore, the patient who suffered was always a slave—hardly the ideal setting for developing fine points of malpractice law. Finally, the doctor himself was often a slave. Too much in the way of training and skill could not be demanded. (This is not to suggest that there might not have been exceptionally gifted slave doctors, but general law looks to the common case.)

The *lex Aquilia* would have handicapped the development of special responsibility in quite a different way. As has been mentioned, for reasons entirely unconnected with the practice of medicine, the statute came to be interpreted very narrowly: there had to be direct physical contact between the body of the injurer and the injured slave. One of the most striking examples that is actually concerned with the practice of medicine, of a midwife, is in *D.9.2.9.pr.*, which has already been quoted. Although in fact in both sets of circumstances, both when there was direct physical contact between the body of the victim and that of the wrongdoer and when there was not, an action would be given, nonetheless concentration on such matters to determine which action actually was available would tend to leave little scope for higher ethical issues.

Such was the liability in delict for medical practitioners and for breaches of professionalism.

Contractual liability has been left to the end because, although it is a very controverted issue for the *artes liberales* and the profession of medicine, the correct answers were, I believe, given long ago by A. Bernard.[47] The relevant texts are few, but the propositions they support are as follows. First, whether or not the practice of medicine was an *ars liberalis*, it was treated as if it were, as the quotation from Cicero *de officiis* 1.51 and from the *Digest*—*D.50.13.1.1*, which is still to come—show. Second, no text shows a freeborn practitioner of an *ars liberalis* suing or being sued concerning professional services on contract, whether on the paid contract of hire (*locatio conductio*) or on the gratuitous contract of mandate (*mandatum*); but several show that the practitioner, if he wanted to sue for remuneration, had to use the extraordinary procedure of *cognitio extraordinaria*. One of these texts specifically mentions doctors:

> D.50.13.1 (Ulpian, *book 8 on All Seats of Judgment*): The governor of a province regularly fixes the law on salaries, but only for teachers of liberal pursuits. We regard as liberal pursuits what the Greeks call *eleutheria*. Rhetors will be included, grammarians, geometers. 1. The claim of doctors is the same as that of professors, unless it is better, since they look after the health of men, the others of their studies. Therefore their legal hearings, too, should be outside the regular system.[48]

The text continues with the same provision for obstetricians and other specialists.[49] Third, when a practitioner of an *ars liberalis* was a slave, his services were governed by a contract of hire made between his master and the other party; hence we can tell that in D.9.2.7.8, the doctor is a slave. When a practitioner was a freedman, his services could be let out by his patron.

It is, I believe, easy to establish the background to these rules. The position is not that professors, doctors, and others did not expect to be paid: the texts show that they did.[50] Rather, in a slave state, work was demeaned: it appeared sordid. Free persons nonetheless had to work, or otherwise pass the time, but there was a psychological need to classify upper-grade pursuits as something different from, and superior to, work: hence the emergence of the liberal arts. But when a slave performed services on his master's behalf for someone else, he worked under a contract—hence the performance of liberal arts by a freeborn person could not be the object of contract. Therefore, such a freeborn person could not be sued for breach of contract. Thus, there could be no contractual action against a freeborn doctor for medical malpractice. This means that there was no standard action available for medical malpractice when the patient was a free person; and when the patient was a slave but the doctor was free, the only standard action was in delict.

The failure of the legal imagination in this case was massive, but it is very understandable. The Roman jurists were never able to separate medical malpractice in the law of delict from its setting-in-life in the realm of damage to property. The decision was made—not very late at that—to separate the "professional" activity of free citizens from the similar labor of slaves, but the distinction never went beyond taking *artes liberales* out of the realm of contract law. No new remedies were created to deal with the *imperitia* or negligence of freeborn, supposedly well-trained, professionals. The Roman failure here, coupled with the power of medical guilds in the Middle Ages and later, has had profound effects on medical malpractice law up to the present day. But that is another story, which will not be told here.

I should like to return to the quotation from Montesquieu. It will be recalled that Montesquieu claimed that Roman statutes punished doctors severely for their negligence or lack of skill. In this I believe he was mistaken. He refers (as well as to the *lex Aquilia*) to the *lex Cornelia de sicariis et veneficiis*. But this piece of Sullan legislation of 81 B.C. concerns murder and similar offenses and nothing is said specifically of doctors,[51] though perhaps under extreme circumstances one might be caught under it.[52] Montesquieu makes an excellent point. It is correct that one should not separate law from the circumstances in which it is made. It was reasonable for him to look for an explanation of the differences in Roman and French law. And, given his theory, it was only to be expected that he would look for the explanation in immediate societal circumstances. To modern eyes, his argument for the differences between Rome and France is prima facie implausible. Yet what other explanation is available in standard sociological terms? The examples he chooses to illustrate his argument show rather that one must look under the surface—or rather that one must look back in time beyond any period when the rules were in existence to find the explanation for them. For medical malpractice in Rome, the action lay in delict under the *lex Aquilia* because it was originally an action for wrongful damage to property; but a contractual remedy scarcely developed for injury to free men because of a desire to distinguish worthy services of free men from those of slaves. France did not receive the *lex Aquilia* and for a long time no satisfactory remedy developed in contract. No provision of the French *code civil* discussed a doctor's liability, and the subsequent case law concerning whether any liability was to be on contract or delict is very illuminating (though it will not be discussed here).

The failure of the Romans to develop medical malpractice law highlights another of their failures: to reform drastically or replace the *lex Aquilia*. Not one text on Chapter 3 concerns the meaning of *frangere* (as distinct from *rumpere*), not one deals with the (obscure) thirty-days rule. Once, for whatever reason, the restricted interpretation requiring for the *actio legis Aquiliae* that the injury be by the body to the body was accepted, there was no further attempt to rationalize the law; and such a distinction, which was not compelled by the wording of the statute and is not found elsewhere, caused at the least complications in the law that later legislation could have rendered unnecessary. At no stage was there ever the slightest sign of juristic (or other) dissatisfaction with the division into Chapter 1 and Chapter 3. Such is the majestic sway of established law over the minds of lawyers. The greatest failure of imagination, of course, was that of those who had control over legislation and did not see, even in the time of Justinian, the need for drastic reform and for replacement of the *lex Aquilia* with a modern statute.

To end on a very different note: the entire theme casts a brilliant light on the pervasive impact of the social institution of slavery. Law, not directly connected with slavery, is distorted by it. Thus, it seems likely that it was because of the money value placed on slaves that no action was easily given for physical injury to a free citizen. Similarly, because the existence of slavery demeans labor, it appears that when the undertakings of freeborn citizens could be classified as *artes liberales*, then they were outside of the realm of contract.

There is an underlying theme in this chapter. Law, as in this case, often grows out of social conditions. But law, once formed, has a life of its own and may continue to keep its original features despite great social changes.

NOTES TO CHAPTER 3

1. 4.3.4.

2. *De l'Espirit des Lois* (first published in 1748), 29.14 He refers to the *lex Cornelia de sicariis* and the *lex Aquilia* (*J*.4.3.7).

3. *Ad legem Aquiliam Liber Singularis.*

4. See, e.g., K. Visky, *Geistige Arbeit und die Artes Liberales in den Quellen des römischen Rechts* (Budapest: Akadémiai Kiádo, 1977), p. 9.

5. It seems reasonable to stress the absence of remedies for breaching a patient's confidences rather than other failures of medical ethics, since Roman attitudes about such matters as a doctor's having sexual relations with a patient could well be different from ours, and the failure of law to develop could lack significance.

6. See J. Scarborough, *Roman Medicine* (Ithaca, N.Y.: Cornell University Press, 1969), pp. 15ff.

7. *De agri cultura*, 156, 157, 158, 159, 160.

8. Ibid., 83, 141, 160.

9. Ibid., 160. At an early date, altars were set up to goddesses for help with childbirth: see Aulus Gellius, *Noctes Atticae* 16.16.4; his information derives from Varro.

10. *De agri cultura*, 83.

11. Pliny, *Historia Naturalis*, 29.6. The account goes back to the antiquarian Cassius Hemina, who lived around the middle of the second century B.C.

12. *D.*33.1.10.3; 34.1.16.1; 38.1.25.2; 38.1.26pr.; 40.5.14.6; see also Varro, *de re rustica* 1.16.4.

13. Cf. *C.*7.7.1.5 (A.D. 530).

14. Si duobus vel tribus hominibus vel pluribus forte optio servi vel alterius rei relicta fuerit, vel si uni quidem legatario optio servi vel alterius rei relicta est, ipse autem moriens plures sibi reliquerit heredes, dubitabatur inter veteres, si inter legatarios vel heredes legatarii fuerit certatum et alter alterum servum vel aliam rem eligere velit, quid sit statuendum. 1. Sancimus itaque in omnibus huiusmodi casibus rei iudicem fortunam esse, sortem etenim inter altercantes adhibendam, ut, quem sors praetulerit, is quidem habeat potestatem eligendi, ceteris autem aestimationem praestet contingentium eis partium: id est in servis quidem et ancillis maioribus decem annis si sine arte sint, viginti solidis aestimandis, minoribus videlicet decem annis non amplius quam decem solidis computandis: sin autem artifices sunt, usque ad triginta solidos aestimatione eorum procedente, sive masculi sive feminae sunt, exceptis notariis et medicis utriusque sexus, cum notarios quinquaginta solidis aestimari volumus, medicos autem et obstetrices sexaginta: eunuchis minoribus quidem decem annis usque ad triginta solidos valentibus, maioribus vero usque ad quinquaginta, sin autem artifices sint, usque ad septuaginta.

15. *De officiis*, 1.150, 151: Iam de artificiis et quaestibus, qui liberales habendi, qui sordidi sint, haec fere accepimus. Primum improbantur ii quaestus, qui in odia hominum incurrunt, ut portitorum, ut faeneratorum. Illiberales autem et sordidi quaestus mercennariorum omnium, quorum operae, non quorum artes emuntur; est enim in illis ipsa merces auctoramentum servitutis. Sordidi etiam putandi, qui mercantur a mercatoribus, quod statim vendant; nihil enim proficiant, nisi admodum mentiantur; nec vero est quicquam turpius vanitate. Opificesque omnes in sordida arte versantur; nec enim quicquam ingenuum habere potest officina. Minimeque artes eae probandae, quae ministrae sunt voluptatum:

Cetarii, lanii, coqui, fartores, piscatores, ut ait Terentius; adde huc, si placet, unguentarios, saltatores totumque ludum talarium.

Quibus autem artibus aut prudentia maior inest aut non mediocris utilitas quaeritur, ut medicina, ut architectura, ut doctrina rerum honestarum, eae sunt iis, quorum ordini conveniunt, honestae. Mercatura autem, si tenuis est, sordida putanda est; sin magna et copiosa, multa undique apportans multisque sine vanitate impertiens, non est admodum vituperanda, atque etiam, si satiata quaestu vel contenta potius, ut saepe ex alto in portum, ex ipso portu se in agros possessionesque contulit, videtur iure optimo posse laudari. Omnium autem rerum, ex quibus aliquid acquiritur, nihil est agri cultura melius, nihil uberius, nihil dulcius, nihil homine libero dignius; de qua quoniam in Catone Maiore satis multa diximus, illim assumes, quae ad hunc locum pertinebunt.

16. *De oratore*, 1.9–11.

17. Ibid., 3.127.

18. *De finibus*, 3.3–5.

19. *Ad familiares*, 13.20. Cicero could also mourn his slave doctor, Alexian, for his kindness and skill: *ad Atticum*, 15.1.1.

20. *De beneficiis*, 6.14.3–16.5:

Illos ex toto praeteribo, quorum mercennarium beneficium est, quod qui dat, non computat, cui sed quanti daturus sit, quod undique in se conversum est. Vendit mihi aliquis frumentum; vivere non possum, nisi emero; sed non debeo vitam, quia emi. Nec, quam necessarium fuerit, aestimo, sine quo victurus non fui, sed quam ingratum, quod non habuissem, nisi emissem, in quo invehendo mercator non cogitavit, quantum auxilii adlaturus esset mihi, sed quantum lucri sibi. Quod emi, non debeo.

"Isto modo," inquit, 'nec medico quicquam debere te nisi mercedulam dicis nec praeceptori, quia aliquid numeraveris. Atqui omnium horum apud nos magna caritas, magna reverentia est.' Adversus hoc respondetur quaedam pluris esse, quam emuntur. Emis a medico rem inaestimabilem, vitam ac bonam valetudinem, a bonarum artium praeceptore studia liberalia et animi cultum; itaque his non rei pretium, sed operae solvitur, quod deserviunt, quod a rebus suis avocati nobis vacant; mercedem non meriti, sed occupationis suae ferunt. Aliud tamen dici potest verius, quod statim ponam, si prius, quomodo istud refelli possit, ostendero. "Quaedam," inquit, "pluris sunt, quam venierunt, et ob hoc aliquid mihi extra pro illis quamvis empta sunt, debes." Primum quid interest, quanti sint, cum de pretio inter ementem vendentemque convenerit? Deinde non emi illud suo pretio, sed tuo. "Pluris est," inquis, "quam venit"; sed pluris venire non potuit. Pretium autem rei cuiusque pro tempore est; cum bene ista laudaveris, tanti sunt, quanto pluris venire non possunt; propterea nihil venditori debet, qui bene emit. . . .Infinitum erit, si latius exempla conquiram, quibus appareat parvo magna constare. Quid ergo? Quare et medico et praeceptori plus quiddam debeo nec adversus illos mercede defungor? Quia ex medico et praeceptore in amicum transeunt et nos non arte, quam vendunt, obligant, sed benigna et familiari voluntate. Itaque, medico, si nihil amplius quam manum tangit et me inter eos, quos perambulat, ponit sine ullo adfectu facienda aut vitanda praecipiens, nihil amplius debeo, quia me non tamquam amicum videt, sed tamquam imperatorem. Ne praeceptorem quidem habeo cur venerer, si me in grege discipulorum habuit, si non putavit dignum propria et peculiari cura, si numquam in me derexit, animum, et, cum in medium effunderet, quae sciebat, non didici, sed excepi. Quid ergo est, quare istis multum debeamus? Non quia pluris est, quod vendiderunt, quam emimus, sed quia nobis ipsis aliquid praestiterunt. Ille magis pependit, quam medico necesse est; pro me, non pro fama artis extimuit; non fuit contentus remedia monstrare: et admovit; inter solicitos adsedit, ad suspecta tempora occurrit; nullum ministerium illi oneri, nullum fasitidio fuit; gemitus meos non securus audivit; in turba multorum invocantium ego illi potissima curatio fui; tantum aliis vacavit, quantum mea valetudo permiserat: huic ego non tamquam medico sed tamquam amico obligatus sum.

21. In general, see K. H. Below, *Der Arzt in römischen Recht* (Munich: Beck, 1953), pp. 22ff.

22.   Ἔϲτιν δὲ καὶ ἐν
ταῖϲ τοῦ Βαϲιλέωϲ Κομμόδου διατάξεϲιν ἐνγεγραμμένον κεφάλαιον ἐξ ἐπιϲτολῆϲ Ἀντωνίνου τοῦ
Εὐϲεβοῦϲ, ἐν ᾧ δηλοῦται καὶ φιλοϲόφουϲ ἀλειτουργηϲίαν ἔχειν ἀπὸ ἐπιτροπῶν. ἔϲτιν δὲ τὰ ῥή-
ματα ταῦτα· ''Ὁμοίωϲ δὲ τούτοιϲ ἅπαϲιν ὁ θειότατοϲ πατήρ μου παρελθὼν εὐθὺϲ ἐπὶ τὴν ἀρχὴν
διατάγματι τὰϲ ὑπαρχούϲαϲ τιμὰϲ καὶ ἀτελείαϲ ἐβεβαίωϲεν, γράψαϲ φιλοϲόφουϲ ῥήτοραϲ γραμμα-
τικοὺϲ ἰατροὺϲ ἀτελεῖϲ εἶναι γυμναϲιαρχιῶν ἀγορανομιῶν ἱερωϲυνῶν ἐπιϲταθμιῶν ϲιτωνίαϲ ἐλαιω-
νίαϲ καὶ μήτε κρίνειν μήτε πρεϲβεύειν μήτε εἰϲ ϲτρατείαν καταλέγεϲθαι ἄκονταϲ μήτε εἰϲ ἄλλην
αὐτοὺϲ ὑπηρεϲίαν ἐθνικὴν ἢ τινα ἄλλην ἀναγκάζεϲθαι''.
See also D.27.1.6.1,9; 50.3.18.30; J.1.25.15; Fragmenta Vaticana, 149.
    23. D.27.1.6.2,10; 50.4.11.3; 50.9.1.
    24. "Beneficia divorum retro principum confirmantes medicos et professores lit-
terarum, uxores etiam et filios eorum ab omni functione et ab omnibus muneribus
publicis vacare praecipimus nec ad militiam conprehendi neque hospites recipere nec
ullo fungi munere, quo facilius liberalibus studiis et memoratis artibus multos insti-
tuant." The rescript is recorded, with variations, in C.10.53(52).6pr.
    25. A. Watson, "Personal Injuries in the XII Tables," Tijdschrift voor Rechtsge-
schiedenis 43 (1975): 213ff.
    26. See, in general, Watson, Law Making, pp. 46ff.
    27. See, e.g., W. M. Gordon, "Dating the Lex Aquilia," Acta Juridica (1976): 315ff.
    28. For this interpretation of triginta diebus proximis, see, above all, D. Daube,
"On the Third Chapter of the Lex Aquilia," Law Quarterly Review 52 (1936): 253ff.
See also, e.g., Watson, Obligations, pp. 236f.; G. Cardascia, "La Portée Primitive de la
Loi Aquilia," in Daube Noster, ed. A. Watson (Edinburgh: Scottish Academic Press,
1976), p. 262.
    29. See above all, Daube, "On the Third Chapter."
    30. See, e.g., Watson, Obligations, pp. 236ff.; Kaser, Privatrecht, 1, pp. 620f.
    31. For the development, see Watson, Obligations, pp. 241ff.; cf. J. L. Barton, "The
lex Aquilia and Decretal Actions," in Daube Noster, at p. 23. Most recently, D. Nörr
holds that originally the verb occidere had the very narrow meaning of "to kill directly" (rather than including "to provide a cause of death") when the lex Aquilia was
passed, probably in the third century B.C.: "Causam Mortis Praebere," in The Legal
Mind, ed. N. MacCormick and P. Birks (Oxford: Clarendon Press, 1986), pp. 203ff. But
he provides no evidence that occidere had in early times such a restricted meaning
and he admits that its meaning was wider by the time Plautus' Pseudolus—see lines
349ff.—was first performed, in 191 B.C. Nor does he explain why this restricted meaning of occidere was retained for the lex Aquilia when in general its meaning (in his
opinion) widened and it was interpreted differently in such other legal contexts as
that of the lex Cornelia de sicariis et veneficiis of 81 B.C. Nor does he explain why a
similarly narrow interpretation was accorded Chapter 3 of the lex Aquilia, where the
word occidere did not occur. Above all, he makes no attempt to show why Republican
texts such as D.9.2.52.2 (and compare 9.2.39pr.) have a wider interpretation than appears to have been the case in the Roman Empire. Indeed, a narrow interpretation
would cause grave injustices if cases of "providing a cause of death" were not given a
remedy. No other remedy is possible before the introduction of ad hoc praetorian
remedies in the late Republic.

32. *D.9.2.9pr.:* "Item si obstetrix medicamentum dederit et inde mulier perierit, Labeo distinguit, ut, si quidem suis manibus supposuit, videatur occidisse: sin vero dedit ut sibi mulier offerret, in factum actionem dandam: quae sententia vera est, magis enim causam mortis praestitit quam occidit."

33. *D.9.2.7pr.*, 4. For our present purposes, we need not consider whether the substance of the texts is interpolated.

34. See, e.g., W. Kunkel, *Herkunft und soziale Stellung der römischen Juristen,* 2nd ed. (Graz: Böhlaus, 1967), pp. 157ff.

35. "Liber homo suo nomine utilem Aquiliae habet actionem: directam enim non habet, quoniam dominus membrorum suorum nemo videtur. . . ."

36. *D.9.1.3* (Gaius, *Book 7 on the Provincial Edict*).

37. See, above all, Lenel, *Edictum,* p. 173.

38. "Ex hac lege iam non dubitatur etiam liberarum personarum nomine agi pose, forte si patrem familias aut filium familias vulneraverit quadrupes: scilicet ut non deformitatis ratio habeatur, cum liberum corpus aestimationem non recipiat, sed impensarum in curatione factarum et operarum amissarum quasque amissurus quis esset inutilis factus."

39. *D.9.4.2pr.*,1 (Ulpian, *book 18 on the Edict*).

40. See, e.g., A. Watson, *Roman Slave Law* (Baltimore: Johns Hopkins University Press, 1987), pp. 68ff.

41. "Imperitia quoque culpae adnumeratur, veluti si medicus ideo servum tuum occiderit, quod eum male secuerit aut perperam ei medicamentum dederit."

42. "Proculus ait, si medicus servum imperite secuerit, vel ex locato vel ex lege Aquilia competere actionem."

43. "Idem iuris est, si medicamento perperam usus fuerit sed et qui bene secuerit et dereliquet curationem, securus non erit, sed culpae reus intelligitur." Cf. *J.4.3.6.*

44. "Mulionem quoque, si per imperitiam impetum mularum retinere non potuerit, si eae alienum hominem obtriverint, volgo dicitur culpae nomine teneri. . . ."

45. Si quis servum conductum ad mulum regendum commendaverit ei, mulum ille ad pollicem suum eum alligaverit de loro et mulus eruperit sic, ut et pollicem avelleret servo et se praecipitaret, Mela scribit, si pro perito imperitus locatus sit, ex conducto agendum cum domino ob mulum ruptum vel debilitatum, sed si ictu aut terrore mulus turbatus sit, tum dominum eius, id est muli, et servi cum eo qui turbavit habiturum legis Aquiliae actionem. mihi autem videtur et eo casu, quo ex locato actio est, competere etiam Aquiliae.

46. *La Responsabilité Médicale* (Paris: Lethielliux, 1968), p. 3.

47. *La Rémunération des Professions Libérales en Droit Romain Classique* (Paris: Domat-Montchrestien, 1936), specifically on medical practitioners from p. 57; cf. Kaser, *Privatrecht,* 1, p. 569.

48. "Praeses provinciae de mercedibus ius dicere solet, sed praeceptoribus tantum studiorum liberalium. liberalia studia autem accipimus, quae Graeci ἐλεγθέρια appellant. rhetores continebuntur, grammatici, geometrae. 1. Medicorum quoque eadem causa est quae professorum, nisi quod iustior, cum hi salutis hominum, illi studiorum curam agant: et ides his quoque extra detur."

49. See also *C.Th.*, 13.3.1.2 (321 or 324), which is repeated at *C.*10.53(52).6.1.

50. See Below, *Der Arzt*, pp. 61ff.

51. See, e.g., T. Mommsen, *Römisches Strafrecht* (Berlin: Duncker & Humblot, 1899), pp. 615ff.; Rotondi, *Leges*, p. 357.

52. L. Kornprost, who seems to follow Montesquieu in this, refers expressly to *D*.48.8.1.1,2 and *D*.48.8.3.1,2,3,5 in *La Responsabilité Médicale* (Paris: Ballière, 1967), p. 26 n.6. But these texts are not concerned with medical practitioners, though they may incidentally be included.

CHAPTER FOUR

OPPORTUNISM AND

PRAGMATISM IN THE LAW

The preceding three chapters stressed failures of the legal imagination, particularly in the realm of lawmaking by legislation. Legislation can be the most drastic, thorough, and comprehensive way of making law. It is also the most "official." But legislators frequently fail to make legislation on private law live up to anything like its potential. Some readers who agree with the particular arguments presented in these chapters may nonetheless think that the chapters give a one-sided argument: the emphasis certainly is on law being out of step with society because it is precisely that situation which needs to be stressed and accounted for in the present state of scholarly analysis. This chapter is intended primarily to show how law might be modified in the absence of appropriate legislation.

Some scholars will maintain, and I am not disposed to disagree, that vigorous legal systems are marked in their development by opportunism and pragmatism, whether by jurist or judge. Major developments often occur through the unexpected use or misuse of existing institutions or by unusual uses of legal argument or by curious borrowings. Here I wish to examine instances from Rome and from the much later Reception of Roman law, where the development was by jurists, and from England, where the development of this kind has been by judges. The phenomenon is, or ought to be, obvious, but I would like also to call attention to some strange mistakes of scholars (especially in Roman law) who ignore or underestimate it.

For Rome, I want above all to discuss the use of *mancipatio*, the ceremony for the transfer of those things which were classified as *res mancipi*. Its form for the classical period is described by Gaius in his *Institutes*, 1.119:

> Now *mancipatio* is, as we said above, a sort of imaginary sale, and it, too, is peculiar to Roman citizens. It is performed thus: not fewer than five witnesses who are Roman citizens above puberty plus one other who holds a bronze scale and is called a *libripens*, are summoned and brought together, and the person who takes by the *mancipatio*, holding the bronze, speaks thus: "I declare this man is mine by the law of the citizens, and let him have been bought by me by this bronze and this bronze scale." Then he strikes the scale with the bronze and he gives the bronze, as if in the place of the price, to the person from whom he is receiving in *mancipatio*.[1]

In *G*.1.121, Gaius tells us that the object to be mancipated must be present, unless it is land, which is regularly mancipated at a distance. The ceremony, whose antiquity is well attested, obviously derives from an actual sale before the time of coined money, when copper or bronze as the price was actually weighed on the scale. Which things were *res mancipi* in Gaius's time are explained by him in *G*.2.14a–17:

> 14a. There is also another division of things: for they are either *res mancipi* or *res nec mancipi*. *Res mancipi* are land and houses on Italic soil, likewise slaves and those animals that are usually broken to draught or burden, such as cattle, horses, mules, and asses: likewise rustic praedial servitudes. For urban praedial servitudes are *nec mancipi*. (15) *Nec mancipi* are also stipendiary or tributary lands. 15. A question is raised as to the meaning of our statement that those animals that are usually broken in are *res mancipi*, because they are not broken in at the time of birth. And the leaders of our school think they are *res mancipi* as soon as they are born. But Nerva and Proculus and other leaders of the other school hold that they do not become *res mancipi* unless they are broken in and if, because of too much wildness, they cannot be broken in then they come to be *res mancipi* when they reach the age at which they usually are broken in. 16. Likewise wild beasts are *res nec mancipi*, such as bears, lions, likewise these

animals which are almost in the category of wild animals, such as elephants and camels; and it does not matter that these animals too are broken in to draught or burden, for their very names did not exist in the time when it was settled which things were *res mancipi* and which *res nec mancipi*. 17. Also *nec mancipi* are almost all incorporeal things, with the exception of rustic praedial servitudes, which, it is settled, are *mancipi* although they are in the category of incorporeal things.[2]

Three peculiarities in the list may help to establish the original list of *res mancipi* and explain the classification. First is the dispute between the Sabinians and the Proculians over cattle, horses, mules, and asses, the Sabinians including all such, the Proculians only those broken in or of the age at which they were usually broken in. Second is the inclusion of land, which is thought not to fit particularly well into the ceremony, which involves a grasping by the hand.[3] Third is the inclusion of rustic praedial servitudes, which were incorporeal rights and did not involve (in classical law at least) the legal right of ownership. A fourth peculiarity—much discussed by scholars and of special interest to Marxists—is less obvious at first sight: the inclusion of horses may be odd, since unlike the other animals classified as *res mancipi*, horses were not much used for agricultural work.[4] Until the invention much later of the horse collar, horses had little pulling power.

But one undoubted fact, as far as I am aware never adduced, may prove helpful—namely that what counted as *res mancipi* would have developed at a very early date, before Rome became a literate society. It appears that "oral cultures tend to use concepts in situational, operational frames of reference that are minimally abstract."[5] Using this notion to guide us, it would appear that (along with slaves) cattle, horses, mules, and asses were all original members of the grouping and that the Proculian view corresponded to the original classification: these were the major animals that worked with man or were worked by man. The Sabinian view that all such animals, whether broken in or not, were *res mancipi* corresponds to the notions of classification of a literate culture.[6]

The remote origins of the classification probably cannot be determined. It may be that originally there was no rigid distinction between *res mancipi* and other things: there was only the feeling that for greater security, important things should be transferred publicly. What these things were gradually became fixed, as did the details of the required ceremony. An alternative thesis might be that some things were conceived of as being more "family" property than other things[7] and were at first inalienable or (both at first and later) alienable only publicly. In either eventuality, slaves, horses, cattles, asses, and mules are an obvious unit. Greater precision is not needed here.

Italic land is also classified as *res mancipi* along with these animate beings, though it is (to us) obviously different in nature. Whether or not it was always so classified—perhaps not, if, as is sometimes claimed, land in early times was not in private ownership—cannot, I think, be established, but the application to it of the ceremony of *mancipatio* is our first glimpse of pragmatism in this context. *Mancipatio*, as a ceremony, involved in its developed form a grasping in the hand that is not entirely appropriate for land. One may conclude either that land was added to the list of *res mancipi* after the form of the ceremony was fixed, or that as the class of *res mancipi* emerged and as the details of the form of transfer were recognized as necessary, one ceremony alone became acceptable for the transfer of all *res mancipi*, though it was not always wholly appropriate. On either view, it was opportunistic either to classify land as *res mancipi* or to treat *mancipatio* as appropriate to it.

But a much more flagrant case of opportunism appears in the classification of rustic praedial servitudes as *res mancipi*.[8] The four original praedial servitudes were *iter*, a right of passage, *actus*, a right of driving beasts, *via*, a right of having a "paved" road, and *aquae ductus*, a right of aqueduct. These servitudes are of extreme economic importance in a primitive agricultural community. Farming neighbors will obviously want to make use of them and they will come into existence in practice by consent, even without legal recognition. But nonetheless the need for legal protection will soon be felt. How are neighbors to create such rights? Some form will be needed. In the absence of official intervention, recourse could be had to the ceremony of *mancipatio*.[9] *Traditio*, the standard method of conveying *res nec mancipi*, could not be used, not just because of its informality, but also because it required physical delivery of the thing to be transferred.[10] There is no alternative to *mancipatio*. And eventually the courts will recognize that servitudes have been created. A purely practical pragmatic solution was found. But, as a consequence, praedial servitudes, though incorporeal rights, were classified as *res mancipi*.

Failure to appreciate Roman legal pragmatism has led most scholars to hold that the early Romans and their successors for a long time conceived of servitudes as corporeal objects, and that the holder of the servitude right had ownership of the corresponding strip of land, or alternatively that ownership of the strip of land was functionally divided between the owner of the land and the neighbor in right of the servitude.[11] Diósdi has given the conclusive arguments against such views by analyzing two provisions of the XII Tables. One provides that the owner of the land must lay a *via* with stones (or, alternatively, set curbstones), and if he does not the other may drive his beast wherever he wants.[12] As Diósdi says, if the person entitled to passage had become the owner of the strip of land, the owner of the servient land would be under no obligation to pave it, nor if the owner failed to do so, would the other be able to lead his beast where he wished.[13] The other provision is even more to the point and declares that the breadth of the *via* should be eight feet on the straight, sixteen feet on the bends.[14] This provision, as Diósdi claims, would have been superfluous if *via* gave ownership, since the transfer itself would then define the territory.[15] It should be stressed that it is the fact that *mancipatio* is used to create servitudes that is the main argument for the belief that servitudes were considered by the early Romans to be corporeal things.

Mancipatio, with a variant wording for the nature of the taking—akin to *fide et fiduciae*, "to my faith and trust"—was used to create real security of *res mancipi*.[16] The creditor accepted ownership of the pledged property, and, since as owner his security was great, he could allow the debtor to continue to possess and use the pledged property.

But the Romans came to use the ceremony of *mancipatio* very creatively well outside the realm of the transfer of *res mancipi*. One early variation was to permit the making of a will. This is described by the jurist Gaius, in the mid-second century A.D., in his *Institutes*, 2.104:

> The proceedings are as follows: the person making the will, as in other mancipations, takes five Roman citizens above puberty as witnesses and a balance-holder and, after having written his will,

mancipates his *familia* [i.e., his property considered as a unit].[17] In the *mancipatio*, the recipient of the *familia* uses these words: "I declare your *familia* and your property to be subject to your instructions under my guardianship so that you may lawfully make a will according to the public statute, and let it have been bought by me with this bronze (and as some add) with this bronze scale." Then he strikes the balance with the bronze and gives the bronze to the testator as if in lieu of the price. Then the testator, holding the tablets of the will, says: "As it is written on these tablets and in this will, so I give, so I legate, so I call to witness, and so, citizens, do you bear me witness." This is called a *nuncupatio, nuncupare* meaning to declare publicly. And by these general words the testator is thought to declare and confirm what he had specifically written in the tablets of the will.[18]

By the second century A.D. (and, indeed, long before), this *testamentum per aes et librum*, as it is called, had become a proper will in which an heir could be appointed. This was not the original position. In early Rome before the XII Tables, a will could be made publicly before the assembly known as the *comitia calata* which met twice a year, on 24 March and 24 May, for the purpose of making wills. This was obviously very inconvenient, and the practice grew up of making testamentary dispositions by using a modified form of *mancipatio*. This practice was confirmed by the XII Tables in a provision (*Tab.* V.3) that read something like: "Uti legassit super pecunia tutelave suae rei, ita ius esto":[19] "As he made a legacy over his property (*pecunia*) and the guardianship of his goods, so let the law be." The provision talks of legating, not of appointing an heir; the word *pecunia*, property, does not have, as *familia* has, the implication of property treated as a unit, and it would thus seem that at that time this type of testamentary disposition did not extend, as it did later, to the appointment of the heir entitled to the estate.[20]

Although no heir could thus be appointed at the time of the XII Tables, this is, nonetheless, a very creative use of *mancipatio*. This variant *mancipatio* could be used to appoint a tutor under the will— a very different result from transferring *res mancipi*—and to transfer *res nec mancipi*. The variant shows that the wording of *mancipatio* was not absolutely fixed and that no real weighing out of copper had to be involved. There is also no evidence that the *familiae emptor* ever acquired any rights or duties as a result of the ceremony,[21] and the legatee became owner automatically on the testator's death. Hence the ceremony did not immediately transfer even *res mancipi* at the moment it was performed. This use seems to have been the result of private initiative, hence the clause confirming its legal effectiveness in the XII Tables.

But scholars seem to have difficulty in accepting the opportunism involved in this kind of development. Thus, M. Kaser talks in terms of a divided ownership between the testator and the *familiae emptor* and subsequently between the *familiae emptor* and the legatees.[22] None of this is justified by the sources, and such an explanation is needed only if one takes a very formalistic attitude to legal development.

A further use of *mancipatio* was in marriage: (*G*.1.113): "By *coemptio* women come into *manus* (matrimonial power) by *mancipatio*, that is by a sort of imaginary sale; thus, in the presence of not fewer than five Roman citizen witnesses above puberty, he, into whose *manus* she comes, buys the woman.[23]

In early Rome, marriage was either *cum manu* or *sine manu*. The former put the wife into the family and under the power of her husband, or of his *paterfamilias* if he had one. The latter left her in her family, or *sui iuris*. *Coemptio* was one of the major ways of putting the wife into the *manus* of her husband, and it existed from an early date. Whether *coemptio* originally was a true sale cannot be established. Certainly one can draw no argument from the fact that the ceremony involved the appearance of a sale, since a similar procedure operated for adoption, which certainly did not involve sale and purchase. In all probability, *coemptio* was a device to extend marriage *cum manu* to segments of the population that could not make use for that purpose of *confarreatio*, which required the presence of some of Rome's highest religious dignitaries, and hence was very much confined to the most powerful families.

One easily overlooked detail in *coemptio* is instructive regarding Roman legal opportunism. There is no indication that *coemptio* was restricted to situations in which a woman had a *paterfamilias*, and it would be very surprising if it were. But if the woman were *sui iuris*, there would be no one for the *familiae emptor* to give the copper to. She would be in the *manus* of her husband and all her property would belong to him, so she should not be the recipient of the copper. The practical Romans were unlikely to have wasted time on such an unimportant technicality.

Closely allied to *mancipatio*, probably in fact a version of it and certainly an act *per aes et libram*, was *nexum*, by which a free man was bound to a creditor and was subject to his control until an amount of bronze that had been paid out was repaid.[24] *Nexum* was regulated by the XII Tables (*Tab.* VI.1), and probably in this context also belongs the provision (*Tab.* IV.2b): "Si pater filium ter venum duit, filius a patre liber esto" ("If a father sells his son three times, let the son be free from the father").[25] If a son was mancipated—that is, given in *nexum*—three times by his father to work off a debt (or until a loan was repaid), the son would become free from paternal power. This clause came to be used very pragmatically to achieve two very different ends. A first pragmatic use was for *emancipatio*, to free a son from paternal power—while his father was still alive— and thus make him a *pater* in his turn. This had numerous advantages for the son, above all in that only a person *sui iuris*, not subject to another's power, could own property:

> G.1.132: Moreover, children cease to be in paternal power by *emancipatio*. But a son passes out from paternal power by three mancipations, other descendants whether male or female by one mancipation. For the XII Tables speak of three mancipations in the case of the son alone, in these words: "If a father sells his son three times, let the son be free from the father." This is the procedure: the father mancipates the son to someone; this last manumits the son *vindicta*; on that account the son reverts into the *potestas* of his father. He mancipates him a second time either to the same or another person (but it is customary to mancipate him to the same person), and he afterward similarly manumits him *vindicta* again; and thereby he reverts again into the *potestas* of the father. The father mancipates him a third time either to the same or another person (but it is customary to mancipate him to the same person) and by this *mancipatio* he ceases to be in the power of the *pater* even though he has not yet been manumitted but is in the position of a *mancipium*.[26]

But, of course, the person who received him by *mancipatio* for the third time would manumit the former son, who now became a *paterfamilias* in his own right. The interpretation of the XII Tables' provision as being restricted to sons—hence other descendants would be free from paternal power after one mancipation—is a minor example of opportunism, intended to simplify the procedure.

The second pragmatic use of the XII Tables clause was to permit adoption of a person who was in *patria potestas:*

G.1.134: Further, fathers cease to have in their *potestas* those children whom they gave to others in adoption. In the case of a son, if he is given in adoption, three mancipations and two intervening manumissions are used, and they are accomplished in the same way as when a father is releasing him from *potestas* in order to make him *sui iuris.* Then either he is remancipated to the father and it is from the father that the adopter claims him as his son in front of the praetor, who, with the father making no counterclaim, adjudges the son to the claimant; or he is not remancipated to the father but the adopter claims him from the person with whom he is under the third mancipation. But remancipation to the father is more convenient. For other descendants whether of the male or female sex one mancipation is enough and either they are or are not remancipated to the father. In the provinces the same proceedings are used before the governor of the province.[27]

We still have not finished with the opportunistic use made by the Romans of the simple ceremony of *mancipatio.* One further use may be adduced. Throughout the classical period,[28] a Roman woman who was *sui iuris* was subject to perpetual tutelage and required the authority of her tutor for various acts. But if she wished a more complaisant tutor, she could, as Gaius tells us (1.115), give herself in *coemptio* with the consent of her tutor, not for the purpose of marriage. The recipient would remancipate her to the person of her choice, whereupon, after being manumitted *vindicta* by him, she would come by matter of law under his tutelage. Until the time of Hadrian, this procedure had a particular advantage, since a woman who had not undergone *capitis deminutio,* or change of civil status, could not make a will:[29]

G.1.115a: Formerly, too, fiduciary *coemptio* was used for the purpose of making a will. For at that time women, with certain exceptions, did not have the right of making wills, unless they had made *coemptio* and had been remancipated and manumitted. But the senate on the authority of the deified Hadrian remitted the need of making a *coemptio.*[30]

The uses made of *mancipatio* represent a splendid success story for legal opportunism. From being a formal, immediate conveyance of certain kinds of things, *mancipatio* became a way to create and transfer easements, to form a real security, to put a wife into the marital power (*manus*) of her husband, to adopt, to free a person from paternal power, to make a will under which even a tutor could be appointed, and to enable a woman to change her status, with the effect, *inter alia*, that she could make a will. But such juristic ingenuity needs official acceptance to be successful. Indeed, for some of the situations involved—notably adoption, emancipation, and the change of a woman's status—active state participation was required.

Opportunism by jurists can go a considerable way at times toward alleviating defects in official lawmaking. But it also pinpoints a particular failure of the legal imagination: that of the state authorities to create the law that was wanted. Successful juristic opportunism can only proceed out of such a failure. But in addition, such successful opportunism shows a readiness on the part of the state authorities to allow others, private individuals at that, to make a considerable part of the private law. Yet the opportunistic uses of *mancipatio* have profound social and economic effects. The creation of legally recognized rustic praedial servitudes allows land to be used much more efficiently; *fiducia* has numerous agricultural and commercial advantages; *coemptio* greatly widens the social range of husbands who have wives in their power, adoption allows families that would otherwise become extinct to continue, emancipation greatly increases the number of persons who can own property, the (more or less) free power of testation is of great consequence for families and dynasties, and so even more is the power of testation accorded to women.

The uses made of *mancipatio* are by no means the only instances of legal opportunism at Rome. Perhaps one other example will suffice, and I wish to choose one that has already surfaced—*manumissio vindicta*. *Manumissio vindicta* existed from the very early Republic and was one of the main ways to manumit a slave; indeed, throughout the classical period, it was the main form of *inter vivos* manumission. A person who wished to free his slave would arrange for a friend to bring against him the *vindicatio in libertatem*, the claim for freedom, before the praetor. The friend thus claimed that a free man was being wrongfully held as a slave, the owner put up no defense, and the praetor declared the slave free.[31] Citizenship was acquired at the same time as freedom. The only other regular means in the Republic and early classical law for *inter vivos* freeing and giving citizenship to a slave was to enroll him on the census as a free man. This may or may not have involved a fiction, but in any event it was excessively inconvenient since the census was taken at most once every five years and after 166 B.C. was largely abandoned.[32]

So much here for ancient Rome. But by far the greatest act of legal opportunism by Western jurists has been the long-extended Reception of Roman law from whenever it might be said to have started until its ending centuries later—if it has yet ended. Without, in most cases, state authorization, jurists in hundreds or even thousands borrowed whatever they thought was suitable, remodeling even that, sometimes with deliberate misinterpretation, to build up a law for their time and place. It is not appropriate here to attempt an account of the process of the Reception. Instead, I want above all to refer to the notion of *Pandektenrecht*, accepted Roman law in Germany in the nineteenth century. It is described thus in the authoritative version of B. Windscheid:

> Under the term "Pandect law" is understood German common law of Roman origin.
>
> German common law is that German private law which operates for Germany as Germany, for Germany as a whole. This German common law is only in part of indigenous origin. For another and overwhelming part it is based on received, foreign, laws and of these Roman law occupies the capital place.
>
> Roman law did not come into force in Germany through an act of legislation, but through the route of customary law and, to be more precise, not through the practice of the people but through the practice of the jurists who made Roman law the foundation of their legal judgments and their legal opinions.[33]

As the passage makes plain, by far the greater part of German common law was of Roman origin, and Windscheid goes on to give as a subsidiary reason for the "Reception" the belief that the Holy Roman Empire was a continuation of the Roman Empire. Of course, German private law at the time was by no means unmodified Justinianic law, but what matters to us above all is, first, that Pandect law was so important in Germany and that it owed its status not to popular use, but to juristic opportunism.

Juristic opportunism and pragmatism, to be successful, must observe certain limits. The jurist must proceed as though his proposition follows from, or can be derived from, existing rules or principles of law, whether or not those principles or rules exist in the jurist's own system or another system to which recourse reasonably can be made.[34] He must argue within the existing legal tradition. The greatest requirement for successful juristic opportunism is plausibility of reasoning or of legal authority. But it is a feature of juristic opportunism that this plausibility need not be more than skin-deep. Provided the jurist gives the appropriate type of argument from existing rules or authorities, his proposition may be acceptable if the legal climate of opinion is right.[35] Nor need his views win acceptance at once.

Likewise, in a legal system in which precedent is granted importance, law may develop through the opportunism and pragmatism of judges (who may, of course, be following a course set by attorneys appearing before them). The major example of this in the Western world is, inevitably, England. For the general proposition, it is enough to quote Milsom: "The life of the common law has been in the abuse of its elementary ideas."[36] Great changes can thus be effected.

To be effective in this regard, both jurists and judges must operate within the rules of the legal game set out for them. Both must achieve the necessary degree of plausibility. But there is a difference here between judge and jurist in that, in general, a higher degree of plausibility is required from a judge: he is sitting in a case in which opposing points of view are urged upon him and, moreover, the judge must make his opinion acceptable at once. Therefore, to be a good judge,[37] the innovator must play down his inventiveness and conceal his art.[38] This emerges clearly from responses to Lord Denning, MR, who does not quite fit the ideal of the innovative judge. That he is the most innovative English judge of this century, no one, I believe, will deny, and he prides himself on this trait.[39] A quotation from one case is enough to establish his approach:

> This brings me to the substantial point in this case. Has there been sufficient claim of maladministration such as to justify investigation

by the commissioner? The governing words of each statute are the same. There must be a written complaint made by or on behalf of a member of the public "who claims to have suffered injustice in consequence of maladministration."

But Parliament did not define "maladministration." It deliberately left it to the ombudsman himself to interpret the word as best he could: and to do it by building up a body of case law on the subject. Now the Parliamentary ombudsman, Sir Edward Compton, has acknowledged openly that he himself gained assistance by looking at the debates in Parliament on the subject. He looked at Hansard and, in particular, at a list of instances of maladministration given by Mr. Crossman, the Lord President of the Council. It is called the "Crossman Catalogue" and is used by the ombudsman and his advisers as a guide to the interpretation of the word. Now the question at once arises: Are we the judges to look at Hansard when we have the selfsame task? When we have ourselves to interpret the word "maladministration"? The construction of that word is beyond doubt a question of law. According to the recent pronouncement of the House of Lords in Davis v. Johnston [1978] 2 W.L.R. 553, we ought to regard Hansard as a closed book to which we as judges must not refer at all, not even as an aid to the construction of statutes.

By good fortune, however, we have been given a way of overcoming that obstacle. For the ombudsman himself in a public address to the Society of Public Teachers of Law quoted the relevant passages of Hansard (734 H.C. Deb., col. 51 [October 18 1966]) as part of his address: and Professor Wade has quoted the very words in his latest book on Administrative Law, 4th ed. (1977), p. 82. And we have not yet been told that we may not look at the writings of the teachers of law. Lord Simonds was as strict upon these matters as any judge ever has been but he confessed his indebtedness to their writings, even very recent ones: see Jacobs v. London County Council [1950] A.C. 361, 374. So have other great judges. I hope therefore that our teachers will go on quoting Hansard so that a judge may in this way have the same help as others have in interpreting a statute.[40]

The reasoning is in proper form for the rules of the judging game. The issue involved the interpretation of statute. Denning seems to accept that to find the meaning one should look for the intention of the legislature, and he appears expressly to acknowledge that, to do so, judges cannot look at legislative history and, in particular, not at Hansard, which gives verbatim the parliamentary debates. In the absence of case law, he is properly prepared to seek nonauthoritative guidance from, as in this instance, the opinion of the ombudsman and academic writing. With regard to the latter, he even cites case law to show that judges may refer to academic opinion. Since the ombudsman and a respected law professor quote the appropriate words from Hansard, he can, he says, take these words into account. Thus, he finds himself able to make use of legislative history. So far, perhaps, so good. The approach is innovative but can be taken as following the cultural rules of judging established by the English judiciary for itself. He accepts the role of legal culture and tradition.[41] But then he pokes gentle fun at the rules of the game: "I hope therefore that our teachers will go on quoting Hansard so that a judge may in this way have the same help as others have in interpreting a statute." He makes it plain to all that he is not only innovating but also is doing so deliberately and that he disapproves of a rule that is so well established that he cannot go directly against it. Nor is this the only occasion when he was cheeky about the nonavailability of Hansard to judges. In *R v. IRC, ex parte Rossminster Ltd.*, he said:

> Beyond all doubt this search and seizure was unlawful unless it was authorised by Parliament. As to the statute, we are not allowed to read Hansard; but you can. You can find it if you turn up the debate. The government of the day put forward the clause. It was opposed by many as being a dangerous encroachment on individual freedom. It was passed by a narrow majority.[42]

And he even refers to the appropriate page in Hansard.

Although many lawyers approve of his innovations, many others are brought close to apoplexy by the fact that he is so blatant about them.[43] Denning prides himself on doing justice in the case immediately before him, regardless of what seems to be the state of the law. Thus, his decisions often seem unprincipled, contrary to principle, and even contradictory.[44] "Good" judges find his approach disturbing. For instance, Lord Scarman writes:

> The question, therefore, arises whether the state of the law which gives rise to such complexities is sound. Lord Denning MR in the Court of Appeal declared that a radical reappraisal of the law is needed. I agree. But I part company with him on ways and means. Lord Denning MR believes it can be done by the judges, whereas I would suggest to your Lordships that such a reappraisal calls for social, financial, economic and administrative decisions which only the

legislature can take. The perplexities of the present case, following on the publication of the report of the Royal Commission on Civil Liability and Compensation for Personal Injury ("the Pearson report") emphasise the need for reform of the law. . . .

Lord Denning MR appeared, however, to think, or at least to hope, that there exists machinery in the rules of the Supreme Court which may be adapted to enable an award of damages in a case such as this to be "regarded as an interim award." It is an attractive, ingenious suggestion, but, in my judgment, unsound. For so radical a reform can be made neither by judges nor by modification of rules of court.[45]

Lord Scarman is a "good" judge. And in the hierarchy of sources of law, the priority of legislation over judicial decision would be generally accepted. But there is a real problem facing the judge and not only for his decision in the instant case. What if, as is argued in this book, the legislature frequently fails in its task to provide appropriate legislation? What if it has failed, moreover, not just in the past, which has given rise to the present case, but is likely to do so in this area of law even for the relatively distant future? And what if the judge's decision is the only plausible way to improve the law, not just for the present case, but also for what is reasonably foreseeable?

NOTES TO CHAPTER 4

1. Est autem mancipatio, ut supra quoque diximus imaginaria quaedam venditio; quod et ipsum ius proprium civium Romanorum est. eaque res ita agitur: adhibitis non minus quam quinque testibus civibus Romanis puberibus, et praeterea alio eiusdem condicionis qui libram aeneam teneat, qui appellatur libripens, is qui mancipio accipit, aes tenens, ita dicit: Hunc ego hominen ex iure quiritium meum esse aio isque mihi emptus esto hoc aere aeneaque libra. deinde aere percutit libram, idque aes dat ei a quo mancipio accipit quasi pretii loco.

2. 14a. Est etiam alia rerum divisio: nam aut mancipi sunt aut nec mancipi. Mancipi sunt velut fundus in Italico solo, item aedes in Italico solo, item servi et ea animalia quae collo dorsove domari solent, velut boves, equi muli, asini; item seruitutes praediorum rusticorum. nam servitutes praediorum urbanorum nec mancipi sunt. (15.) item stipendiaria praedia et tributaria nec mancipi sunt. 15. Sed quod diximus ea animalia quae domari solent mancipi esse, quomodo intellegendum sit quaeritur, quia non statim ut nata sunt domantur. et nostrae quidem scholae auctores statim ut nata sunt mancipi esse putant; Nerva vero et Proculus et ceteri diversae scholae auctores non aliter ea mancipi esse putant quam si domita

sunt, et, si propter nimiam feritatem domari non possunt, tunc videri mancipi esse incipere, cum ad eam aetatem pervenerint qua domari solent. 16. Item ferae bestiae nec mancipi sunt, velut ursi, leones, item ea animalia quae fere bestiarum numero sunt, velut elephanti et cameli; et ideo ad rem non pertinet quod haec animalia etiam collo dorsoue domari solent; nam ne nomen quidem eorum animalium illo tempore fuit, quo constituebatur quasdam res mancipi esse, quasdam nec mancipi. 17. Item fere omnia quae incorporalia sunt nec mancipi sunt, exceptis servitutibus praediorum rusticorum; nam eas mancipi esse constat, quamvis sint ex numero rerum incorporalium.

3. See, e.g., H. F. Jolowicz and B. Nicholas, *Historical Introduction to the Study of Roman Law,* 3rd ed. (Cambridge: Cambridge University Press, 1972), p. 138.

4. See, e.g., P. Vigneron, *Le Cheval dans l'antiquité Gréco-Romaine* (Nancy: Faculté des Lettres et des Sciences Humaines de l'Université, 1968), pp. 139ff.; K. D. White, *Roman Farming* (London: Thames & Hudson, 1970), pp. 288ff. Some use of horses was, however, made by farmers. See Cato, *de agri cultura,* 138.

5. W. J. Ong, *Orality and Literacy* (London: Methuen, 1982), p. 49. Ong gives the following example for preliterate classification:
Subjects were presented with drawings of four objects, three belonging to one category and the fourth to another, and were asked to group together those that were similar or could be placed in one group or designated by one word. One series consisted of drawings of the objects *hammer, saw, log, hatchet.* Illiterate subjects consistently thought of the group not in categorical terms (three tools, the log not a tool) but in terms of practical situations—"situational thinking"—without adverting at all to the classification "tool" as applying to all but the log. If you are a workman with tools and see a log, you think of applying the tool to it, not of keeping the tool away from what it was made for—in some weird intellectual game. A 25-year-old illiterate peasant: "They're all alike. The saw will saw the log and the hatchet will chop it into small pieces. If one of these has to go, I'd throw out the hatchet. It doesn't do as good a job as a saw" (1976, p. 56). Told that the hammer, saw, and hatchet are all tools, he discounts the categorical class and persists in situational thinking: "Yes, but even if we have tools, we still need wood—otherwise we can't build anything" (ibid.). Asked why another person had rejected one item in another series of four that he felt all belonged, he replied "Probably that kind of thinking runs in his blood."
Ong, *Orality,* p. 51. The example is taken from A. R. Luria, *Cognitive Development: Its Cultural and Social Foundations* (Cambridge, Mass.: Harvard University Press, 1976), p. 56.

6. Earlier, I took the view that one could not determine whether the Sabinian or the Proculian view corresponded to the original classification: *XII Tables,* pp. 136f. Elephants and camels would not be included because they were not known or used by the Romans when the classification became fixed.

7. See, e.g., P. Bonfante, *Corso di diritto romano, 2, La proprietà* (Rome: Società editrice del foro italiano, 1927), p. 182; for a different opinion see, e.g., G. Diósdi, *Ownership in Ancient and Preclassical Roman Law* (Budapest: Akadémiai Kiádo, 1970), pp. 22ff.

8. G.2.14a, 17.29; *Epitome Ulpiani,* 19.1; *Vaticana Fragmenta,* 45.

9. *In iure cessio,* which in any event is cumbersome, is unlikely to have existed so early: see, e.g., Watson, *Property,* p. 93 and especially n.1.

10. G.2.19: of Buckland, *Textbook of Roman Law,* 3rd ed. by P. Stein (Cambridge: Cambridge University Press, 1963), pp. 226f.

11. For the extensive literature, see Diósdi, *Ownership,* pp. 109ff.

12. Festus, *s.v. viae: Tab.* vii.7.

13. Diósdi, *Ownership*, p. 114.

14. *D*.8.3.8; *Tab*. vii.6.

15. Diósdi, *Ownership*, p. 114.

16. For the argument, see Watson, *Obligations*, pp. 72ff.; cf. Kaser, *Privatrecht*, 1, p. 460.

17. For the argument see Watson, *XII Tables*, p. 57.

18. Eaque res ita agitur: qui facit <testamentum,> adhibitis, sicut in ceteris mancipationibus, v testibus civibus Romanis puberibus et libripende, postquam tabulas testamenti scripserit, mancipat alicui dicis gratia familiam suam. in qua re his verbis familiae emptor utitur: FAMILIAM PECUNIAMQUE TUAM ENDO MANDATELA TUA CUSTODELAQUE MEA <ESSE AIO, EAQUE,> QUO TU IURE TESTAMENTUM FACERE POSSIS SECUNDUM LEGEM PUBLICAM, HOC AERE (et ut quidam adiciunt) AENEAQUE LIBRA ESTO MIHI EMPTA. deinde aere percutit libram, idque aes dat testatori velut pretii loco. deinde testator tabulas testamenti tenens ita dicit: HAEC, ITA UT IN HIS TABULIS CERISQUE SCRIPTA SUNT, ITA DO, ITA LEGO, ITA TESTOR, ITAQUE VOS QUIRITES TESTIMONIUM MIHI PERHIBETOTE; et hoc dicitur nuncupatio. nuncupare est enim palam nominare; et sane quae testator specialiter in tabulis testamenti scripserit, ea videtur generali sermone nominare atque confirmare.

19. *Epitome Ulpiani*, 11.14; cf. *D*.50.16.53*pr*. Rather different versions appear in Cicero, *de inventione* 2.50, 148 (cf. *Rhetorica ad Herennium*, 1.13.23) and *G*.2.224 (cf. *D*.50.16.120). For the argument establishing Ulpian's as the original version, see Watson, *XII Tables*, p. 52.

20. See Ibid., p. 52 for the full argument.

21. See Ibid., p. 64 for the argument.

22. *Privatrecht*, 1, p. 108 and the authors he cites. Against the notion of divided ownership see above all Diósdi, *Ownership*, pp. 121ff.; and Watson, *XII Tables*, pp. 125ff. Most recently, Kaser defended his view of relative ownership and divided ownership in "Relatives Eigentum," *ZSS* 102 (1985): 1ff. P. Birks, "The Roman Law Concept of *Dominium* and the Idea of Absolute Ownership," *Acta Juridica* (1985): 1ff., says nothing à propos.

23. "113. Coemptione uero in manum conueniunt per mancipationem, id est per quandam imaginariam venditionem. nam, adhibitis non minus quam V testibus civibus Romanis puberibus, item libripende, emit is mulierem cuius in manum convenit." Cf. *G*.1.123; Boethius, *II in Topica Ciceronis*, 3.14; Servius, *in Vergilii Georgicon*, 1.31; Isidorus, *Etymologiae*, 5.24; Nonius Marcellus, *s.v. Nubentes*.

24. *Nexum* itself may, but need not, be an opportunistic use of *mancipatio* so will not be dealt with here, but see Watson, *XII Tables*, pp. 111ff.

25. For the argument, see Ibid., pp. 118f. The provision involved *mancipatio* (or no opportunistic use of the provision could have been made for *mancipatio*), but no real sales (or the son would not have returned to the *potestas* of the father).

26. 132. Praeterea emancipatione desinunt liberi in potestate parentum esse. sed filius quidem tribus mancipationibus, ceteri vero liberi sive masculini sexus sive feminini una mancipatione exeunt de parentium potestate. lex enim XII tabularum tantum in persona filii de tribus mancipationibus loquitur his verbis: Si pater filium <ter> uenum duit, a patre filius liber esto. eaque res ita agitur: mancipat pater filium filium alicui; is eum vindicta manumittit; eo facto revertitur in potestatem patris; is eum iterum mancipat vel eidem uel alii (sed in usu est eidem mancipari), isque eum postea similiter vindicta manumittit; eo facto rursus in potestatem patris revertitur; tertio pater eum mancipat vel eidem uel alii (sed hoc in usu est, ut

eidem mancipetur), eaque mancipatione desinit in potestate patris esse, etiamsi nondum manumissus sit, sed adhuc in causa mancipii. . . .

27. 134. Praeterea parentes eos liberos in potestate habere desinunt quos aliis in adoptionem dederunt. et in filio quidem, si in adoptionem datur, tres mancipationes et duae intercedentes manumissiones proinde fiunt, ac fieri solent cum ita eum pater de potestate dimittit ut sui iuris efficiatur. deinde aut patri remancipatur, et ab eo is qui adoptat vindicat apud praetorem filium suum esse, et illo contra non vindicante <a> praetore vindicanti filius addicitur, aut non remancipatur patri, sed ab eo vindicat is qui adoptat, apud quem in tertia mancipatione est. sed sane commodius est patri remancipari. in ceteris vero liberorum personis seu masculini seu feminini sexus una scilicet mancipatio sufficit, et aut remancipantur parenti aut non remancipantur. eadem et in provinciis apud praesidem provinciae solent fieri.

28. See, e.g., Buckland, *Textbook*, p. 165.

29. See, e.g., *G*.1.115; 2.112; Cicero, *topica*, 4.18; A. Watson, *Persons*, pp. 152f.

30. 115a. Olim, etiam testamenti faciendi gratia fiduciaria fiebat coemptio. tunc enim non aliter feminae testamenti faciendi ius habebant, exceptis quibusdam personis, quam si coemptionem fecissent remancipataeque et manumissae fuissent. sed hanc necessitatem coemptionis faciendae ex actoritate divi Hadriani senatus remisit.

31. See, e.g., *G*.1.17.

32. See, e.g., A. Watson, *Roman Slave Law* (Baltimore: Johns Hopkins University Press, 1987), pp. 24f.

33. *Lehrbuch des Pandektenrechts*, 9th ed. (Frankfurt am Main: Rütten & Loenig, 1906), pp. 1f.

34. For a jurist to be opportunistic is not the same as being inventive or innovative. A jurist may propose an innovation and demonstrate its advantages, but unless he attaches the proposition to existing modes of legal reasoning, its acceptance will depend either on legislation or on later changed attitudes.

35. Thus, J. Voet supported the proposition that drunkenness bars agreement in sale unless the intention continues, with three Roman texts—*D*.48.19.11.2; *J*.2.11.1; and *D*.50.17.48—none of which concerned a sale or other contract and only one referred to drunkenness: *Commentarius ad Pandactas*, 18.1.4; for the absence of Roman law on the subject, see A. Watson, "Drunkenness in Roman Law," in *Sein und Werden im Recht*, ed. W. G. Becker and L. Schnorr v. Carolsfeld (Berlin: Duncker & Humblot, 1970), pp. 301ff. Again, the medieval development of a delict remedy for disfigurement is based on Roman sources that had no such meaning: see, e.g., R. Feenstra, "The Historical Development of Delictual Liability for Killing and the Infliction of Bodily Harm," *Acta Juridica* (1972): 235.

36. *Foundations*, p. 6. For examples see throughout that work.

37. See, e.g., A. Watson, "A House of Lords' Judgment, and Other Tales of the Absurd," *American Journal of Comparative Law* 33 (1985): 673ff.

38. David Daube points out that when a judge, for corrupt reasons, wishes to innovate, he or she must be particularly subtle: "A Corrupt Judge Sets the Pace," in *Gedächtnisschrift f. Wolfgang Kunkel*, ed. D. Nörr and D. Simon (Frankfurt am Main: Klostermann, 1984), pp. 37ff.

39. See, e.g., Lord Denning, *The Discipline of Law* (London: Butterworths, 1979), *passim*.

40. *Regina v. Local Commissioner, Ex parte Bradford Council (C.A.)*, p. 287 at pp. 311f.

41. On this see Watson, "Judgment."

42. 1979 3 All E. R. 385 at 399: cf. M. Zander, *The Law Making Process*, 2nd ed. (London: Weidenfeld and Nicolson, 1985), p.119.

43. See above all the opinions in the essays in *Justice, Lord Denning and the Constitution*, ed. P. Robson and P. Watchman (London: Gower, 1981), and *Lord Denning: The Judge and the Law* ed. J. L. Jowell and J. P. W. B. McAuslan (London: Sweet & Maxwell, 1984).

44. See, e.g., P. S. Atiyah, in *Lord Denning: The Judge and the Law* at p. 30.

45. *Lim Poh Choo v. Camden and Islington Area Health Authority* [1979] 2 All ER 910 at 913f. See also his remarks in *Associated Newspapers Group v. Wade* [1980] I.C.R. 161 at 189f.

CHAPTER FIVE

NATURAL LAW AND ENGLISH

LEGAL POSITIVISM

In this chapter, I wish to discuss a very different kind of failure of the legal imagination: that of legal philosophers. I will briefly maintain that the main strand of modern English legal philosophy—positivism as exemplified by John Austin, *The Province of Jurisprudence Determined* (1832), and Herbert Hart, *The Concept of Law* (1961)—is not concerned with the major issues of the nature of law. My main aim, though, is to show first how it comes about that scholars of that eminence can concentrate on relatively unimportant and formal issues, which they nonetheless regard as of central interest to legal philosophy.

A subsidiary aim is to add a fresh dimension to my often-repeated argument that legal development—in the broadest sense of law: the structure of the system, its major divisions, the approach to the sources of law, and the legal rules themselves—owes a great deal to the legal tradition and, to a marked degree, is independent of social, political, and economic factors.

The argument for holding that mainstream legal positivism concentrates largely on side issues is easily set down. Positive law cannot be an end in itself. It is and can only be a means to an end. And this, of course, is seen by Austin and Hart. I would submit that theories of the nature or concept of positive law that then exclude consideration of the content of law, what law does, what law can do, the ends to which law is a means, and how positive law is used to achieve the ends, fail at the outset to address any of the important issues. Yet Austin and Hart—as well as Hans Kelsen, *The Pure Theory of Law*[1]—exclude such considerations from the core of their work.[2]

Again, obedience to law seems deeply relevant to the nature of law, and it does appear prominently in the theory of Austin. But the reason for obedience is not worked out even there, and no sustained attempt is made to find a conceptual link between law and obedience to law; nor is the nature of any obligation to obey law satisfactorily investigated.[3] To this I will return. The issue here is not whether Austin, Kelsen, and Hart are powerful thinkers or whether the answers they give are correct.[4] It is whether the questions to which they give answers are important or central ones about the nature of law (or the nature of positive law). The issue is not, for instance, whether positive law can be correctly regarded as a union of primary and secondary rules, but whether, if law can be so regarded, we have learned the most significant things about the nature or concept of law. The answer suggested above is negative.

It would, I believe, be generally admitted that for modern British legal positivism the seminal work is Austin's *The Province of Jurisprudence Determined*. Thus, Hart has shown a great deal of interest in Austin—for instance, he wrote an introduction to a 1954 edition[5]—and it is reasonable to regard *The Concept of Law* as taking Austin's book as the point of departure for Hart's own theory and as an attempt to avoid Austin's errors and provide fresh and more satisfactory solutions to Austin's concerns. Indeed, in the 1954 introduction, Hart criticized Austin for not using the fundamental notion of rule in his analysis of positive law, and it is there that Hart produced and enlarged on his own major theorem: "A legal system is a system of rules within rules."

Austin's position is well known. It is briefly set down here as a preliminary to showing that it is intimately linked with a preceding tradition in which the questions asked about the nature of law were central to law and fundamental.

Austin may be said to have defined human positive law, properly so called, as the command of a sovereign backed by a sanction; and by definition, a sovereign is one whose commands are habitually obeyed and who is not himself in a habit of obedience to a determinate human superior. God's positive commands are his law, properly so called, but they are distinct from human positive law, and conceptually they are not linked. Within this framework, it is very difficult to fit custom—and consequently international law or primitive law—as law properly so called.

For the preceding tradition I will begin arbitrarily but appropriately with the Spanish theologian and Jesuit, Francisco Suárez (1548–1617). Any starting point for this tradition—as for many others—would be arbitrary, but for our purposes we need begin not necessarily at the beginning but only at a time when, I believe, the tradition was satisfactory in the sense of asking and trying to answer the central questions. Moreover, Suárez was a superb philosopher.

The first book of Suárez's work, *De Legibus, ac Deo Legislatore* (1612), is entitled "On Law in General; and on its Nature, Causes and Effects." In it, Suárez accepts the necessary existence of God and asserts, appropriately for the time but also expressly, the creation of rational creatures. Then:

> The argument can be adduced from the very fact that an intellectual being has been created that he has a superior to whose forethought and order he is subject; and because he is intellectual he is capable of moral government, which occurs through command. Therefore it is connatural and necessary to such a being that he be subject to some superior by whom he is ruled by command or law.[6]

Suárez proceeds to divide law into categories, above all, following Plato, into divine, celestial (which, in effect, he rejects as unnecessary), natural, and human law.[7] A subsequent category is positive law:

> With regard to the other division of law, the positive, one must note that the term *positive* is applied to that law which is not inherent in nature nor in grace, but has been laid down in addition to them by an extrinsic principle endowed with power, wherefore it is called "positive," having been added, as it were, to the natural law, not flowing therefrom of necessity. . . .[8]

> Thus the theologians deduce a third division, that of positive law, into divine and human. That positive law is called divine which has been

established directly by God Himself and added to the whole body of natural law. Of human positive law, we shall speak presently.[9]

A little further on in the same chapter, he discusses human law specifically:

Thus it is called human law because it was found and established proximately by men. I say, however, proximately because every human law derives ultimately in some way from the eternal law; as it is said, "Through me kings rule, and the creators of law decree justly" (Proverbs 8); and, as to the binding force of such law, that flows from the power given by God because "There is no power unless from God" (Romans 13). . . . And elsewhere (in John's Gospel, tractate 6) he [i.e., St. Augustine] says that God distributed human laws to the human race through rulers.[10]

In the next section, Chapter 18, Suárez says that from what has gone before the necessity for human law is apparent, because natural or divine law contains only certain self-evident principles of behavior. In Chapter 19, he claims, relying on Plato and St. Thomas (whom he has quoted), that it is possible to explain more fully the necessity involved:

The necessity is founded in this, that man is a social animal, demanding the civil life and communication with other men; and hence it is necessary that he live rightly, not only as he is a private person but also as he is a part of the community; and this above all depends on the laws of the individual community.[11]

Subsequently Suárez considers whether law is an act of the intellect or of the will and he decides in favor of the latter because of characteristic properties of law: "The third property we were to discuss was that law orders, but this most properly pertains to the will."[12]

He also claims that four characteristic conditions necessary to law are found in an act of the will rather than in an act of the intellect. The first three—the fourth can be left aside here—are the following: "The first is moving and bringing the subject person to perform the action, understanding always in the term action also omission. . . . The second is to be in possession of binding force. . . .

The third is that lawmaking is an act of the jurisdiction and power of a superior."[13] Thus, the important notion of a sanction for disobedience to the law is brought into account. But it is not made a central element of law, nor does Suárez claim that every law must have a sanction. After giving the four characteristic conditions—which incidentally show that he is thinking of a territorial ruler—he adds a final argument: "For the will which the superior has of compelling the subject to such an act or—what is similar—of bringing such matter within the necessary boundaries of virtue is very much appropriate to the designation of law."[14]

In the subsequent chapter, Suárez discusses whether it is in the nature of law to be established for a community, and he replies in the affirmative. He then divides communities into kinds. One kind of community is natural, which is brought about solely by its members possessing a rational nature, is the community of humankind, and to this community pertains natural law: "Another kind may be called a political or mystical community through a special conjunction in a congregation that is morally a union."[15] Communities of this type may be considered an offshoot of natural communities and may be regarded as comprising additions to nature, brought about by divine law, and they are, namely, formerly the Jewish synagogue and now the Catholic church.[16] It is for this sort of community that, by their very nature, divine positive laws primarily were made. For the rest, some communities are perfect, others imperfect, and as an example of the latter he gives a private household:

> One reason, of course, is that such a community is not self-sufficient as will be at once explained. Likewise because in it the individual persons are not congregated as principal members to constitute one political body, but only exist therein as inferiors for the benefit of the master, and to the extent that they are, in some sense, subjected to his dominion. And so such a community *per se* and within its proper bounds is governed not by a true power of jurisdiction but by a power of domination, and so for the diversity of dominion it partakes of a different measure of dominion with respect to diverse persons. For there is one right or dominion of the *paterfamilias* over his wife, another over sons, another over servants or slaves. Nor does it, properly speaking, partake of a political government, and so that community is simply called imperfect.[17]

Human laws should be framed only for perfect communities, and every perfect community is a true political body governed by means of its own jurisdiction, which has a coercive force, namely legislation.[18] The most obvious example of a perfect community is the territorial state, but it is not the only one; a religious community or a confraternity or similar group may also be a perfect community.[19]

In the following chapter, Suárez argues that it is inherent in the nature of law that it be enacted for the common good.[20] Further on, he argues that it is inherent in the nature of law that it prescribe just things and that it be justly established.[21] With regard to the inherent nature of law to prescribe just things, he argues:

> With regard to human laws, this is based on a different principle. For the human legislator does not have a perfect will, as God does, and therefore, insofar as it comes from him and with regard to the act prescribed he can sometimes prescribe unjust things; as is agreed. But he does not have the power to create a binding obligation through unjust laws, and therefore although he prescribes unjust things such prescriptions are not law, because he lacks the power or validity to bind. I am speaking of unjust acts that are contrary to natural or divine law. For if an act is wicked solely because it is prohibited by human law, and it (i.e., the law) can be removed by a subsequent law, then this second law will not be about evil deeds, because, once the first law has been revoked, the evil of the deed is removed. Thus, the reason for our assertion becomes clear first because that power came from God. But the things that are from God are well ordered; therefore it is given for good and for instruction, not for evil or for destruction. Then secondly, no inferior can create a binding obligation contrary to law and to the will of his superior. But a law prescribing an evil act is contrary to the law of God who forbids it. Therefore it cannot create a binding obligation because it is impossible for men at the same time to be bound to do and not do something.[22]

Subsequently, in the second book Suárez argues that human law is an effect of eternal law: human law, as existing in its author, is law by participation in the eternal; it emanates from a power given by God; it has binding force insofar as it depends upon principles of the eternal law; and finally, for human law to be righteous it should conform to eternal law.[23]

Eventually, but still in book 1, he gives his definition of law: it "is a common precept, just and stable, and sufficiently promulgated."[24]

The second book of this work is entitled "On the Eternal Law and Natural Law and the *ius gentium.*" He argues for the necessary existence of the eternal law and discusses its nature. He does the same for natural law and also argues that natural law is binding in conscience.[25] He goes on to discuss *ius gentium,* a difficult notion in view of the various meanings given to the term. Very generally— sufficient for our purposes—Suárez may be said to use *ius gentium* primarily to mean international law. He claims that it differs from natural law mainly in that, insofar as it contains precepts, it does not derive the necessity for them from a manifest inference from natural principles.[26] In fact, he says, *ius gentium* is human and positive, though it does, of course, differ from civil law. The precepts of the *ius gentium* exist through the customs, not of one or two nations, but of all or nearly all nations.[27]

Books 3 to 8 deal with human positive law: in particular, book 7 deals with custom. Book 9 concerns the old positive divine law, and book 10, the last, the new divine law.

Of course, Suárez's work contains a great deal more than has been set out here, but enough has been said, I believe, for our purposes. Suárez offers a comprehensive theory of law embracing eternal, divine, natural, and human law. He offers a definition of law sufficiently wide—much too wide in absolute terms, modern jurists might claim—to embrace all these varieties of law; and he has no problem in fitting within his definition both customary law and international law. Nonetheless, the reader (I hope) is struck by an emphasis on elements that recur in or perhaps cause difficulty for Austin.

Above all, Suárez's approach stresses law as the will or command of a superior. That is inevitable for him, given his starting point, and the idea is central to any natural law theory that has a theological basis: man is created by God, therefore man is inferior to God and ought to obey his commands: since man is created as a rational being, he is capable of moral government through commands. The obligation to obey God's law is a moral one. The same idea is central—and appropriately so—for Suárez's view of human positive law; God created man as a social and intelligent being who lives fully only in society; for peaceful organized life, God created rulers for society, and their precepts are law and to be obeyed; these human laws are only directly created by man because ultimately they are from God (who created man, who must live in society, with rulers, rulers themselves created by God, who make law as a result of their power that emanates from God). Thus, human laws are binding on political inferiors. But it must be emphasized that for Suárez the compelling element in human law is not just a sanction—though the idea of enforcement underlies much of what he says. Rather, the main compelling element is that human laws are binding on con- science: there is necessarily a moral obligation to obey God, the creator and superior—hence rules established by those he has ap- pointed to rule are themselves binding, as his orders at one remove, on the political inferiors of the rulers.

The moral content of precepts proposed by human rulers is of fundamental importance in the theory. Human rulers, being imper- fect, may establish precepts to commit evil. But such precepts are not law—first, because human rulers' power derives from God, but what derives from God is well ordered and is not given for evil; sec- ond, because the human ruler is the inferior of God and, as an in- ferior, cannot make valid laws contrary to those of his superior (such human precepts, accordingly, are not binding). The first argument may not appeal to modern lawyers, but the second is a very proper and acceptable legal argument that follows from Suarez's original assumption.

Suárez may stand as an outstanding example of an author of a natural law theory of law based on theology (or on divine revelation) in the Western tradition. That his influence, direct and indirect, on subsequent jurists was great cannot seriously be doubted. Some of the ideas expressed in his account of law were already well estab- lished; where he was original, his ideas passed into common cur- rency, at least for discussion. He was, for instance, a major influence on Hugo Grotius's *De Jure Belli ac Pacis,*[28] though he is cited there but four times. That work is singled out because it is widely re- garded as the starting point—at least it was the first seminal work— of a fresh school of natural law (hereinafter termed "the law of rea- son") that sought to establish the nature of law by reference to the nature of man as a social and rational animal, and by avoiding re- course to arguments based on religion.

The person chosen to exemplify this school is Samuel Pufendorf (1632–1694), a central figure at all times in this tradition, and who occupied the first chair set up for the teaching of natural law and international law (specifically Grotius, *De Jure Belli ac Pacis*) at Heidelberg in 1661. He, I will maintain and hope to demonstrate, imbued in the legal tradition, was thoroughly immersed in the ideas to be found in Suárez, modified them in the light of current preoccupation and scholarship, and adopted them within the framework of the law of reason.

The nature of the present claim should be spelled out. I am not claiming that Pufendorf took Suárez, and only Suárez, as his starting point, and that variations between Suárez and Pufendorf are the result of a direct rejection of the former by the latter, and of intellectual innovations by the latter. The historical position is much more complicated: views found in Suárez, even when original to him, are found in many other writers; innovations or changes that are responses to arguments or positions found in Suárez may be found in writers prior to Pufendorf. Rather, the two jurists are chosen here because they represent two outstanding figures in this legal tradition—a legal tradition that to some extent had split, but where the writings of the later jurist, Pufendorf, taken as representing the law of reason, clearly demonstrate the impact on it of the theological law of nature, as represented by Suárez. It would presumably be possible, but difficult and unnecessary here, to trace through various personages the descent of the various strands of thought. It would be difficult because often (as in Pufendorf) references to previous jurists are not given and unnecessary because the broad sweep of the impact is obvious when Pufendorf is compared with Suárez. But it is well known that the first draft of Pufendorf's early work *Elementorum Jurisprudentiae Universalis Libri Duo* (which will primarily be considered here) was written when he was imprisoned in 1658 and had no access to learned books.

Pufendorf offers a definition of law: "A law is a decree by which a superior binds someone subjected to him to direct his actions according to the superior's command."[29] And he explains his definition. Law is to be distinguished from a counsel, pact, and a right.[30] Law does not involve free choice on the part of the person bound:

> But in the one who is going to pass a law for another it is above all required that he have such power over the person on whom the law will be imposed that he can compel him to observe the law by a

115

penalty that is proposed. For it is pointless to order something which can be neglected with impunity. Therefore no one is bound by the laws of a person or a group which does not have power over him.[31]

Who has such power seems in this work simply to be whosoever has such power: "And the faculty of imposing something by means of law or precept implies superiority just as the obligation of obeying indicates that we are inferior to him who can compel us, at least so far as his command extends."[32] Elsewhere in the same book, he writes:

> The nature of law consists above all in this that it is a notional norm for actions showing how far they should conform to the will of some superior. I use the term *notional norm* because it touches actions only notionally, in representing to the intellect the will of the superior with regard to something which ought to be done or not done. For when this is made known an obligation immediately arises in the subject to act in accordance with that law. And that for this reason; he who enjoined the law on him has the power to compel him by the imposition of some evil, if he fails to obey. It is established that he will use this power from the fact that no one is presumed to wish his action to be without effect.[33]

The subject has an obligation to obey the law, the reason being, we are told, that the legislator has the power to impose a penalty. Thus, the obligatory force of law resides in its sanction. There seems, however, to be a flaw in Pufendorf's argument. Fear of the sanction may be a reason for obedience but it does not on that account entail an obligation. If a gunman threatens to shoot me if I refuse to hand over my wallet, I have a reason for obeying him, but no one, I think, would say I have an obligation to obey him.[34] In his *De Officio Hominis et Civis libri duo*, however, Pufendorf claims that obligation is properly introduced into the mind of a man by a superior—that is, a person who not only has the power to bring some harm on those who resist but also has "just causes for his claim to circumscribe the freedom of our will at his choice." These just causes are conspicuous benefits given to the person obligated; or if it is shown that the superior wishes the person obligated well and can better look out for him than that person can for himself, and has also actually claimed control over him; and lastly if one

116

person gave himself into the control of another.[35] In the absence of a just cause, when fear is removed nothing remains to prevent the subject from following his own wishes.

In the *Elementa* Pufendorf also discusses natural law, and his treatment does contain references to God and divine revelation:[36]

> With regard to their authors a division of law can be made into *divine* and *human*. Divine law, on the ground of promulgation can again be divided into *natural* or general and *positive* or special. All human law is *civil*. With regard to substance some things clearly are in harmony with the very condition of human nature, and flow from it. Some things, however, arise from the sole will of the legislator, as if from a particular status of men. Of these the first are called natural, the latter positive.[37]

According to this, natural law is part of divine law, but the substance of some human law may be natural in this sense, although all human law (unlike all of divine law) is promulgated. God's positive law, Pufendorf insists, cannot be contrary to natural law because natural law is also God's law. When civil law conflicts with the law of nature, no obedience, he asserts, is due to the state: "But if, however, a state, by means of a precept and with threat of punishment, binds its subject to do or not do something which the law of nature forbids or enjoins, we emphatically deny that obedience is owed to it."[38]

He again discusses the sanction for a law, and it is clear that for him a sanction is an essential element in law. As he puts it clearly in *De Officio:*

> There are two parts of any perfect statute: one in which is defined what is to be done or omitted: the other in which it is shown what punishment is proposed for one who ignores the command and does the forbidden. For, on account of the wickedness of the human spirit, attracted to the forbidden, it is pointless to say "Do this" if there is no punishment in store for one who does not do it; it is also absurd to say "You will pay the penalty" unless the reason that deserves the punishment has preceded. Thus, all the force of a law consists in showing what the superior wished or did not wish to be done by us and what penalty was established for violation of the law. But the power to impose an obligation, that is to impose an intrinsic necessity, and the power of compulsion or by imposing penalties forcing one to

observation of the law, properly resides in the legislator and in him to whom the keeping and execution of the law is committed.[39]

Pufendorf rejects the notion that there is any law of nations or international law, except insofar as it is the same as the law of nature.[40] In this context, he does not seem to regard custom as law. He says that civilized nations have tempered the harshness of war:

> Hence come customs regarding the exemption of certain things and persons from the force of war, fixed ways of injuring enemies, ways of treating prisoners, and such like. If one, waging legitimate war, neglects such things—of course when that can properly be done by the law of nature—he can be said to have contravened no valid obligation; he will only be commonly accused of barbarity, because he did not conform himself to the customs of those who number war among the liberal arts. . . . Therefore if he wages just wars he can conduct them according to the law of nature alone, nor is he bound by any law to these customs unless he wishes of his own free will on account of some gain.[41]

The clear—and, I believe, correct—implication is that Pufendorf does not regard custom as creating law in the field of international relations. Indeed, he seems not to regard custom anywhere as law. His definition is of *lex*, law in the sense of statute. The term *ius*, which has a variety of meanings, is used by other writers at times to mean law in general, including statutes. But this would not seem to be Pufendorf's usage, especially when he writes of positive law. He says expressly that *ius* is often used with the same meaning as *lex*, especially when it is used regarding a complex of *leges*, statute law (in general). The other meaning of *ius*, which he distinguishes, is that of a right.[42] For him, law is statute law. There is a further implication in the passage. If in failing to observe the accepted customs of war (which are not part of natural law) a prince behaves barbarously, he has not breached a valid obligation. The implication is that law contains an obligation of obedience (though, one must add, only when human positive law is not contrary to natural law).

Thus, important elements of Suárez's theory of law reappear in Pufendorf, to such an extent that, I believe, the great dependence of Pufendorf on the tradition to which Suárez belonged cannot be denied. There is no element in Pufendorf's definition that is not explicit in the theory of Suárez. But Pufendorf's theory is very much thinner. Although theology is not absent from Pufendorf, he does not base his theory on the existence of God or His creation of man. His definition of law belongs to the tradition that gave Suárez his starting point: law is the command of a superior. But whereas for Suárez the obligation to obey was based on conscience, and there was a moral obligation (there being a clear system of rightful command from God to the superior to the inferior), for Pufendorf the reason for obedience to human law is simply to avoid the punishment that the superior can at will inflict.

Admittedly, Pufendorf in *De Officio* talks of "just causes" that give the superior the right to punish for breaches of an obligation "properly introduced," but this view appears to be an afterthought and is not attractively worked out. Pufendorf's definition makes central and essential to law the existence of a sanction, which was not so stressed and was not central to Suárez. Pufendorf's breaking away from the theological notion of the superior has a further consequence: for Pufendorf, the identity of the superior is a practical issue; it is he who can impose the sanction. There is thus no apparent need, as there was for Suárez, for the superior to be a political superior, the leader of a perfect community (whether the community is a territorial state or something else). Again, for Suárez, legislation was but one of the sources of law, but his starting point in the creation of man as a social animal by God, with rulers established by God, meant inevitably that legislation would feature prominently in his treatment of law, especially in the opening book. Pufendorf's definition is so colored by this approach that it can apply only to statute, and this involves a view of law as restricted to statute. Without any express discussion of the subject, custom as a source of law disappears. When custom as law goes out, so does international law as law.

But Pufendorf's insistence that natural law is law means that his definition does take at least some account of the content of the law: a human statute conflicting with natural law does not impose an obligation of obedience. But he seems not to deny the statute the status of law (though he seems not to accord it expressly, either).

A further weakness in Pufendorf must be stressed. Pufendorf insists that there is a conceptual link between law, including human law, and the obligation of obedience. But the obligation, as we have seen, is the result of the sanction: he does not also argue for a further moral obligation to obey law. Yet he asserts—without producing arguments—that there is no obligation to obey human law when it is contrary to natural law. But obviously the human sanction remains even when the human law is contrary to natural law; and it is this sanction that Pufendorf uses as the basis of the obligation to obey human law. If the sanction is there for all human law, what happens to the obligation to obey law? It seems to hang in the air, with no justification.

Pufendorf's centrality to the law of reason is beyond question. And his influence was enormous. For almost two centuries—to speak in minimum terms—his works were prescribed texts in a great many universities in Europe and beyond, notably in North America.

To see the impact on legal theory of the combined strands of thought in Suárez and Pufendorf it is enough to look almost at random at one much later work on the civil law written for Catholic seminarists in Italy (in the seminary at Reate) at the request of a bishop, namely C. Latino, *Iuris Civilis Elementa ad usum Reatini seminarii* (Reate, 1830). At 1.2.1 Latino defines *Lex*: "Praeceptum commune, rationabile, natura sua perpetuum, a Summo Imperante latum, et sufficienter promulgatum, obligans, Subditos, ud ad eius normam suas actiones componant" ("A general precept, reasonable, perpetual by its nature and passed by the supreme authority, binding subjects to regulate their behavior according to his role").

As Pufendorf's definition of law depends on the tradition of Suárez, so—though even more clearly—does Austin's theory depend on the tradition of Pufendorf.

As Pufendorf removes the theological underpinnings from the older tradition, so does Austin remove the natural law or law of reason content from Pufendorf's view of law. Weaknesses that had been introduced into the truncated theory of law as represented by Pufendorf were either retained by Austin and remain as weaknesses in his theory, or they impelled him to try to make improvements.

A weakness that obviously had to be dealt with was Pufendorf's notion of a superior. Clearly not everyone who could enforce his will by threat of punishment should be regarded as a superior who could legislate, and presumably Pufendorf himself, if he had had to face the issue, would not have made so wide a claim. Indeed, when he discusses the superior, he writes as though he is thinking of a political superior.[43] Austin expressly restores the notion of the superior as the political superior, the sovereign; and he offers as the marks of sovereignty the following:

> 1. The *bulk* of the given society are in a *habit* of obedience or submission to a *determinate* and *common* superior; let that common superior be a certain individual person or a certain body or aggregate of individual persons. 2. That certain individual, or that certain body of individuals, is *not* in a habit of obedience to a determinate human superior.[44]

Austin concentrates on positive law and in particular on human positive law, and so natural law drops out. With it disappears the idea of any necessary conceptual link between law and morality:

> The existence of law is one thing; its merit or demerit is another. Whether it be or be not is one enquiry; whether it be or be not conformable to an assumed standard, is a different enquiry. A law, which actually exists, is a law, though we happen to dislike it, or though it vary from the text, by which we regulate our approbation and disapprobation. This truth, when formally announced as an abstract proposition, is so simple and glaring that it seems idle to insist upon it. But simple and glaring as it is, when enunciated in abstract expressions the enumeration of the instances in which it has been forgotten would fill a volume.
>
> Sir William Blackstone, for example, says in his "Commentaries," that the laws of God are superior in obligation to all other laws; that no human laws should be suffered to contradict them; that human laws are of no validity if contrary to them; and that all valid laws derive their force from that divine original. . . .[45]
>
> But the meaning of this passage of Blackstone, if it has a meaning, seems rather to be this: that no human law which conflicts with the Divine law is obligatory or binding; in other words, that no human law which conflicts with the Divine law *is a law*, for a law without an obligation is a contradiction in terms. I suppose this to be his meaning, because when we say of any transaction that it is invalid or void, we mean that it is not binding: as, for example, if it be a contract, we mean that the political law will not lend its sanction to enforce the contract.

Now, to say that human laws which conflict with the Divine law are not binding, that is to say, are not laws, is to talk stark nonsense. The most pernicious laws, and therefore those which are most opposed to the will of God, have been and are continually enforced as laws by judicial tribunals. Suppose an act innocuous, or positively beneficial, be prohibited by the sovereign under the penalty of death; if I commit this act, I shall be tried and condemned, and if I object to the sentence, that it is contrary to the law of God, who has commanded that human lawgivers shall not prohibit acts which have no evil consequences, the Court of Justice will demonstrate the inconclusiveness of my reasoning by hanging me up, in pursuance of the law of which I have impugned the validity. An exception, demurrer, or plea, founded on the law of God was never heard in a Court of Justice, from the creation of the world down to the present moment.

But this abuse of language is not merely puerile, it is mischievous. When it is said that a law ought to be disobeyed, what is meant is that we are urged to disobey it by motives more cogent and compulsory than those by which it is itself sanctioned. If the laws of God are certain, the motives which they hold out to disobey any human command which is at variance with them are paramount to all others. But the laws of God are not always certain. All divines, at least all reasonable divines, admit that no scheme of duties perfectly complete and unambiguous was ever imparted to us by revelation. As an index to the Divine will, utility is obviously insufficient. What appears pernicious to one person may appear beneficial to another. And as for the moral sense, innate practical principles, conscience, they are merely convenient cloaks for ignorance or sinister interest: they mean either that I hate the law to which I object and cannot tell why, or that I hate the law, and that the cause of my hatred is one which I find it incommodious to avow. If I say openly, I hate the law, *ergo*, it is not binding and ought to be disobeyed, no one will listen to me; but by calling my hate my conscience or my moral sense, I urge the same argument in another and more plausible form: I seem to assign a reason for my dislike, when in truth I have only given it a sounding and specious name. In times of civil discord the mischief of this detestable abuse of language is apparent. In quiet times the dictates of utility are fortunately so obvious that the anarchical doctrine sleeps, and men habitually admit the validity of laws which they dislike. To prove by pertinent reasons that a law is pernicious is highly useful, because such process may lead to the abrogation of the pernicious law. To incite the public to resistance by determinate views of *utility* may be useful, for resistance, grounded in clear and definite prospects of good, is sometimes beneficial. But to proclaim generally that all laws which are pernicious or contrary to the will of God are void and not to be tolerated, is to preach anarchy, hostile and perilous as much to wise and benign rule as to stupid and galling tyranny.[46]

Blackstone seems to talk of the obligation to obey law: "the laws of God are superior in obligation to all other laws"; "human laws are of no validity if contrary to them." That is, he denies an obligation to obey human law that is contrary to divine law. Austin contradicts this and says, "for a law without an obligation is a contradiction in terms." Thus, for Austin there exists an obligation to obey law.[47] But how does he prove that there is an obligation to obey human law? By pointing to the sanction that will be imposed by the human superior in the event of disobedience, Austin does not here go beyond Pufendorf.

Austin distinguishes positive law properly so called from positive moral rules that are laws improperly so called, that is, "laws set or imposed by general opinion." What prevents these positive moral rules from becoming laws properly so called is the absence of a sovereign issuing a command. On this basis, international law is only positive morality:

> The positive moral rules which are laws improperly so called, are *laws set* or *imposed by general opinion:* that is to say, by the general opinion of any class of any society of persons. For example, some are set or imposed by the general opinion of persons who are members of a profession or calling: others, by that of persons who inhabit a town or province: others, by that of a nation or independent political society: others, by that of a larger society formed of various nations.
>
> A few species of the laws which are set by general opinion have gotten appropriate names.—For example, There are laws or rules imposed upon gentlemen by opinions current amongst gentlemen. And these are usually styled *the rules of honour,* or *the laws* or *law of honour.*—There are laws or rules imposed upon people of fashion by opinions current in the fashionable world. And these are usually styled *the law set by fashion.*—There are laws which regard the conduct of independent political societies in their various relations to one another: Or, rather, there are laws which regard the conduct of sovereigns or supreme governments in their various relations to one another. And laws or rules of this species, which are imposed upon nations or sovereigns by opinions current amongst nations, are usually styled *the law of nations* or *international law.*
>
> Now a law set or imposed by general opinion is a law improperly

so called. It is styled a *law* or *rule* by an analogical extension of the term. When we speak of a law set by general opinion, we denote, by that expression, the following fact:—Some *indeterminate* body or *uncertain* aggregate of persons regards a kind of conduct with a sentiment of aversion or liking: Or (changing the expression) that indeterminate body opines unfavourably or favourably of a given kind of conduct. In *consequence* of that sentiment, or in *consequence* of that opinion, it is likely that they or some of them will be displeased with a party who shall pursue or not pursue conduct of that kind. And, in *consequence* of that displeasure, it is likely that *some* party (*what* party being undetermined) will visit the party provoking it with some evil or another.[48]

This is akin to Pufendorf's notion of international law as custom (when it is not the same as the civil law of individual nations or part of the law of nature).

Austin's theory obviously owes a great deal to the natural law theory of which Pufendorf is a representative. He has sharpened the notion in Pufendorf of the human superior or sovereign, but otherwise there is nothing basic in Austin that is not to be found in Pufendorf. Austin has cut out natural law and retained only positive law, both divine and human. But for Austin, as for Pufendorf, divine positive law and human positive law are not conceptually linked. Austin's theory is thus a direct descendant, by way of the law of reason, of the tradition, developed by theologians and legal scholars, of the laws of God and man as exemplified by Suárez. Austin, indeed, has scarcely improved on Suárez's idea of a human superior or sovereign or on his ideas of the commands of a human sovereign. As the quotations from Suárez show, he was well aware of the nature and characteristics of what Austin calls positive law properly so called, though he had a different view of their validity. Indeed, Austin cannot be understood except in connection with natural law predecessors; and it is his dependence on their theories, as altered by himself and others, that accounts for the deficiencies in his theory.

The failure of the legal imagination of the positivists results from their removing elements from earlier theories without realizing that the fragment left cannot bear its own weight. Human positive law (in Austin) is in effect reduced to statute; judicial lawmaking can only be accommodated in the most artificial way, and customary law and international law not at all. Law entails an obligation to obey it, but the nature of the obligation is without foundation. The link between morality and law is broken, perhaps rightly so; but in consequence the positivist theory of law excludes consideration of the content of law. The fact that law is a means to an end and cannot be an end in itself, though recognized, is lost sight of. What law does and can do, and how it does what it does, are left aside.[49] My quarrel is not so much with the logic of positivism as with its thinness in the Austinian formulation.[50]

A person who stands some little way outside a tradition is better able to judge the impact of the tradition than one in the thick of it. One can see how one thought leads to another and can appreciate the way in which the thrust of an argument is altered to take account of some objection. One can also see how, in changed circumstances, one standpoint can continue to predominate. One may also see that those at work in the tradition are so involved with it that they are blind to the attractions of other approaches; what can be regarded as of interest is circumscribed by the past concerns of those working in the tradition. In the present context, the fascinating aspect of the working out of the tradition is not any sharpening of the idea of human positive law and the ever-increasing separation of it from the laws of God and the laws of nature (and the decline of interest in these). Rather, it is the failure to consider human positive law from a fresh standpoint, or alternatively to treat the establishment of the concept of human positive law as merely the preliminary, though necessary, first step to discussing the nature of law.

We now return for a final look, from a different angle, at legal positivism and at John Austin in particular. A fundamental difficulty exists for legal positivists if they wish to claim that there exists an obligation to obey law (though some deny that there is any such obligation[51]). And, as we have seen, such a claim is inherent in Austin. But he never seems to clarify the nature of this obligation, except for insisting that there will be a sanction in the event of disobedience.[52] This, however, constitutes a reason for obedience but not an obligation to obey. But if there is an obligation to obey law, it cannot be a legal obligation. As Peter Singer puts it, because legal obligations derive from law, there would have to be a law obliging one to obey that law. But then there would have to be a law obliging one to obey the obliging law. There would then be an infinite progression.[53] In the final analysis, any obligation to obey law, if there is one, must stand outside this positive legal system.

Hence, any obligation to obey law because it is law must be an obligation lying outside of the law itself. No such obligation can be accepted by any theory of positive law. It may therefore be an attraction—not a weakness—of natural law theories that they insist on an obligation to obey law that exists outside the man-made legal system.

For positivists, the only way out of this dilemma would seem to be to deny the existence of any obligation to obey law because it is law. But then since law to be law must have some element of effectiveness, the positivists would have to claim that there was no conceptual link between law and the obligation to obey but that there was between law and the fact of obedience. And then the nature both of this fact of obedience and also of its conceptual link with law would have to be explained.

As an addendum, something should be said about the views of recent writers on Austin regarding the influences on the main outlines of his legal thought as presented here. Much is rightly made of his relationship to Jeremy Bentham.[54] As for foreign influences, the stress is on the time the Austins spent in Bonn and the knowledge John Austin gained of Roman law and the German Historical School.[55] F. J. C. Hearnshaw emphasizes personal factors, such as his early career as an army officer:

> Soon his military experiences faded into the dim, indefinite background of his life; but they probably impressed upon his mind a permanent tendency to over-emphasise the element of command in law, and to stress unduly the indivisible and illimitable character of supreme authority. His jurisprudence always smacked of the drill-sergeant.[56]

The traditions represented by Suárez and Pufendorf are neglected. Neither of these writers is mentioned by either of the two recent biographers of Austin, W. L. Morison and W. E. Rumble.[57] Andreas Schwarz mentions Pufendorf, but only to contrast him with the current of thought in Germany with which Austin became acquainted.[58] Hearnshaw mentions Suárez in passing, but not to link his theory with Austin's.[59,60]

NOTES TO CHAPTER FIVE

1. (Berkeley: University of California Press, 1978); from the second German edition.

2. Austin especially does show that he wishes positive law to conform to the values of utilitarianism: *The Province of Jurisprudence Determined*, lectures 3, 4, 5. But this still tells us nothing significant about the content of law, what law does or can do, or how the ends of law are achieved.

3. See P. Soper, *A Theory of Law* (Cambridge, Mass.: Harvard University Press, 1984), pp. 30ff.

4. Furthermore, the issue is not whether in works other than those mentioned these jurists have made important contributions to legal thinking.

5. In the "Library of Ideas" series (London: Weidenfeld & Nicolson, 1954).

6. "[D]eclarari potest, quia intellectualis creatura eo ipso, quod creatura est, superiorem habit, cuius providentiae, et ordini subiaceat, et quia intellectualis est, capax est gubernationis moralis, quae fit per imperium; ergo connaturale est, ac necessarium tali creaturae, ut subdatur alicui superiori, a quo per imperium seu legem regatur." From *De legibus, ac Deo legislatore*, 1.3.3.

7. *De legibus*, 1.3.5.

8. Ibid., 1.3.13: "Circa alterum membrum de lege positiva sciendum est, illam legem vocari positivam, quae non est innata cum natura, vel gratia, sed ultra illas ab aliquo principio extrinseco habente potestatem posita est; inde enim positiva dicta est, quasi addita naturali lege, non ex illa necessario manans."

9. Ibid., 1.3.14: "Atque hinc traditur a Theologis tertia divisio legis positivae in divinam, et humanam. Lex positiva divina dicitur, quae ab ipso Deo immediate lata est, et toti lege naturali addita; de humana statim dicemus."

10. Ibid., 1.3.17:
Dicitur ergo humana lex, quia proxime ab hominibus inventa, ac posita est. Dico autem proxime, quia primordialiter omnis lex humana derivatur aliquo modo a lege aeterna; iuxta illud. Per me Reges regnant, ac legum conditores iusta decernunt. Proverb 8 ac quoad vim obligandi manat a potestate Deo data, quia non est potestas, nisi a Deo. *Rom 13*. . . . Et tract. 6 in Ioan, dicit Deum per imperatores distribuisse humano generi iura humana: 1.3.17.

11. Ibid., 1.3.19: "Nam in hoc fundatur, quod homo est animal sociabile, natura sua postulans vitam civilem, ac communicationem cum aliis hominibus, ac ideo necesse est ut recte vivat, non solum ut privata persona est, sed etiam ut est pars communitatis; quod ex legibus uniuscuiusque communitatis maxime pendet."

12. *De legibus*, 1.5.13: "Erat tertia proprietas, quod lex ordinat, at hoc proprissime convenit voluntati."

13. Ibid., 1.5.15: "Prima est movere, ac applicare subditum ad exercendam actionem, sub actione semper omissionem intelligendo . . . Secunda est, habere vim obligandi. . . .Tertia, ferre legem est actus iurisdictionis ac potestatis superioris."

14. Ibid., 1.5.16: "Nam illa voluntas, quam superior habet obligandi subditum ad talem actum, vel (quod perinde est) constituendi talem materiam intra necessarios terminos virtutis optime recipit denominationem legis."

15. Ibid., 1.6.18: "Alia vero dici potest communitas politica, vel mystica per specialem coniunctionem in congregatione morali modo una."

16. Ibid., 1.6.18.

17. Ibid., 1.6.20:

Ratio vero est, quia illa communitas non est sibi sufficiens, ut statim explicabitur; Item quia in ea non congregantur singulae personae ut principalia membra ad unum corpus politicum componendum, sed solum ibi existunt inferiores in utilitatem Domini, ac quatenus eius dominio aliquo modo subsunt. Et ideo talis communitas per se loquendo, ac inter proprios terminos non regitur propria potestate iurisdictionis, sed dominativa, atque ita pro diversitate dominii participat diversum modum imperandi respectu diversorum. Aliud enim est ius, vel quasi dominium patris familias in uxorem, aliud in filios, aliud in famulos, vel servos; unde neque habet perfectam unitatem, seu uniformem potestatem; neque etiam participat proprie politicum regimen, et ideo communitas illa simpliciter imperfecta dicitur.

18. Ibid., 1.6.21.

19. Ibid., 1.6.19.

20. Ibid., 1.7.

21. Ibid., 1.9.

22. Ibid., 1.9.4:

De legibus autem humanis, hoc fundatur in alio principio. Nam legislator humanus non habet voluntatem perfectam, sicut Deus ac ideo quantum est ex se, ac quoad factum potest interdum iniqua praecipere, ut constat; non tamen habet potestatem ad obligandum per iniquas leges, ac ideo licet iniqua praecipiat, tale praeceptum non est lex, quia vim, aut valorem ad obligandum non habet; loquor autem de opere iniquo, quod fit contra legem naturalem, aut divinam. Nam si malum solum quia prohibitum lege humana, ac illa possit auferri per subsequentem legem, iam illa posterior lex non erit de opere malo, quia, revocata priori lege, tollitur malitia operis. Et ita est clara ratio assertionis, tum quia illa potestas est a Deo; quae autem a Deo sunt, ordinata sunt, ergo est data in bonum, ac in aedificationem, non in malum, seu in destructionem. Tum etiam quia nullus inferior potest obligare contra legem, ac voluntatem superioris: sed lex praecipiens pravum actum est contra legem Dei prohibentis illum: ergo non potest obligare, quia impossibile est, homines simul obligari ad agendum, ac non agendum aliquid.

See also 1.1.6.

23. Ibid., 2.4.8.

24. Ibid., 1.12.5: "Lex est commune praeceptum, iustum, ac stabile sufficienter promulgatum."

25. Ibid., 2.5–14.

26. Ibid., 2.19.2.

27. Ibid., 2.19.6.

28. See, e.g., J. B. Scott in *Selections from Three Works of Francisco Suárez*, II, trans. G. L. Williams et al. (Oxford: Clarendon Press, 1944), pp. 17ff. Although the translations in this chapter are my own, I express a great indebtedness to the above-mentioned work.

29. *Elementa* 1, def. 13: "Lex est decretum, quo superior sibi subjectum obligat, ut ad istius praescriptum actiones suas dirigat."

30. Ibid., def. 13.1ff.; see also *De Jure Naturae et Gentium Libri Octo*, 1.6.1.

31. Ibid., def. 13.4:

In eo autem, qui legem alteri laturus est, praeprimis requiritur, ut in illum, cui iniugenda lex, habeat potestatem talem, qua possit poena proposita ad observantiam legis illum adigere: nam frustra est aliquid praecipere, quod potest impune negligi. Inde nemo obligatur legibus personae aut coetus alicujus, cui in ipsum nihil sit potestas.

32. Ibid., def. 13.4: "Et facultas iniugendi aliquid per modum legis aut praecepti infert superioritatem: quemadmodum obligatio parendi arguit inferiores nos esse eo, qui praecipere nobis potest, saltem qua imperium ejus se extendit."

33. Ibid., def. 13.9:

Consistit aurem natura legis potissimum in hoc, ut sit norma notionalis actionum, quatenus ad voluntatem superioris alicujus debent formari. Dico norma notionalis, quia ad actiones duntaxat concurrit notionaliter, dum intellectui repraesentat voluntatem superioris circa aliquid agendum aut omittendum. Haec enim ubi innotuit, statim in subdito exoritur obligatio juxta legem illam faciendi. Idque; quia intelligit, eum qui istam injungit, potestatem habere detre ctantem malo imposita adigendi; quam potestatem actu eum exseriturum inde constat, quod nemo actionis suae nullum este effectum velle praesumatur.

34. See H. L. A. Hart, *The Concept of Law* (Oxford: Clarendon Press, 1966), pp. 80f.

35. *De Officio*, 1.2.5.

36. *Elementa* 1, def. 13.6ff.

37. Ibid., def. 13.13:

Divisio legum respectu autorum fieri potest in divinam et humanam: divina ratione promulgationis iterum in naturalem seu generalem, et positivam seu peculiarem dispescitur. Lex humana omnis civilis est. Quantum autem ad materiam, quaedam cum ipsa humanae naturae qua talis, conditione manifeste congruunt et ex ea fluunt; quaedam autem ex solo arbitrio legislatoris, tanquam peculiariter certo hominum statui congruentes oriuntur: quarum illae naturales, hae positivae vocantur.

38. Ibid., def. 13.7: "Quod si tamen civitas per modum praecepti et cum comminatione poenae subjectis suis injungant aliquid agendum, aut intermittendum, quod lex naturae interdicit aut praecipit, ei heic obsequium deberi pernegamus."

39. *De Officio*, 1.2.7:

Cujuslibet legis perfectae duae partes sunt: una per quam definitur quid sit faciendum, quidve omittendum: altera per quam indicatur, quodnam malum sit propositum ei, qui praeceptum intermittit, ac interdictum facit. Nam uti propter pravitatem ingenii humani, in vetita tendere amantis supervacuum est dicere, hoc fac, si non faciendum nil mali sit mansurum: ita absurdum est dicere poenas dabis, ni causa, quae poenam mereatur, praecesserit. Sic igitur omnis vis legis consistit in significando eo, quid superior a nobis fieri velit ac quae poena violatoribus legis sit constituta. Vis autem obligandi, i.e., intrinsecam necessitatem adferendi ac vis cogendi, seu per poenas ad observationem legum adigendi proprie est in legislatore, ac cui legum custodia atque exsecutio est commissa.

40. *Elementa* 1, def. 13.24.

41. Ibid., def. 13.25:

Unde consuetundines circa exemptiones certarum rerum ac personarum a vi bellica, modus nocendi hostibus, modus tractandi captivos, ac similia. Quae si quis legitimum gerens bellum neglexerit, scilicet ubi per jus naturae recte fieri possunt, nulli obligationi validae contravenisse dici potest, nisi quod ruditas vulgo arguitur, quia non ad consuetudinem eorum, queis bellum inter artes liberales numeratur, sese composuerit ... Igitur si quis justa gerat bella, solo naturae iure ea regere potest, nec ullo iure ad istas consuetudines, nisi sponte ob commodum aliquod suum velit, tenetur.

42. Ibid., def. 1.13.3.

43. Ibid., 13.10.

44. *The Province of Jurisprudence Determined*, lecture 6 (in the 1954 edition, pp. 193f.).

45. Ibid., p. 184.

46. Ibid., pp. 185f.

47. My friend Neil MacCormick disagrees with me and holds that neither Austin nor Hart assumes an obligation to obey law. On the passage just quoted from Austin, he writes: "He does not say that there is an obligation to obey law. He says that if laws require act A, then *eo ipso* it is obligatory to do A." For my view that Hart assumes an obligation to obey law, I would call attention to his distinction between the gunman whose threat obliges and the taxman whose threat obligates: *The Concept of Law*, pp. 80f. What is the nature of this distinction if the law creates no obligation of obedience? See Soper, *A Theory of Law*, pp. 30f. See also Hart, *The Concept of Law*, p. 168. He talks of "legal rules of obligation" that we "conceived as binding independently of the consent of the individual bound."

48. *The Province of Jurisprudence*, lecture 5 (in the 1954 edition, pp. 140f.).

49. In addition, and on a very different level, such theories of positive law cannot include as an integral part any theory of the nature of human society. Hence they cannot, and do not, include any discussion of the legitimacy of the sovereignty. Whether the sovereign obtained his power by force or retains it by fraud is irrelevant as long as his commands are habitually obeyed. Law is reduced to one aspect of political power. Moreover, such theories cannot include within themselves any obligation on the sovereign to make moral law.

50. See, e.g., Hart, "Positivism and the Separation of Law and Morals," *Harvard Law Review* 71 (1958): 593ff.

51. See, e.g., J. Raz, *The Authority of Law* (Oxford: Clarendon Press, 1979), pp. 233ff.

52. *The Province of Jurisprudence*, lecture 6 (in the 1954 edition, pp. 184ff.).

53. P. Singer, *Democracy and Disobedience* (Oxford: Clarendon Press, 1973), p. 3. Positivists are, of course, aware of the problem and may claim that the progression or spiral is broken where there is official acceptance or recognition of the obligation. But, then, how is one to identify the official? For one attempt at solving the problem see N. MacCormick, *Legal Reasoning and Legal Theory* (Oxford: Clarendon Press, 1978), pp. 53ff.

54. See, e.g., the numerous references to Bentham in W. L. Morison, *John Austin* (Stanford, Calif.: Stanford University Press, 1982) and in W. E. Rumble, *The Thought of John Austin* (London and Dover, N.H.: Athlone Press, 1985).

55. See, e.g., Andreas B. Schwarz, "John Austin and the German Jurisprudence of His Time," *Politica* 1 (1934): 178ff.; Morison, *John Austin*, pp. 60ff.; Rumble, *The Thought of John Austin*, pp. 31f.

56. *The Social and Political Ideas of Some Representative Thinkers of the Age of Reaction and Reconstruction* (London: Harrap, 1932), p. 163.

57. See Morison, *John Austin*; Rumble, *The Thought of John Austin*; nor are they mentioned by Julius Stone in his analytical treatment of Austin's thought: *Legal System and Lawyers' Reasoning* (Stanford, Calif.: Stanford University Press, 1964), pp. 63–97.

58. Schwarz, "John Austin," p. 184.

59. Hearnshaw, *Social and Political Ideas*, p. 173.

60. The original impetus for this chapter came from a discussion many years ago with my friend John L. Barton. See A. Watson, *The Nature of Law* (Edinburgh: Edinburgh University Press, 1977), p. 130 n. 19.

CHAPTER SIX

SOME LEGAL PHENOMENA

Sadly, if my views on legal development and change, on the relationship between private law and society, as set out in the preceding chapters and elsewhere, are deemed correct, then I will have succeeded in making law and society and legal evolution very "unsexy" subjects. One will not be able to claim that law mirrors life, that law is "the spirit of the people," or that law typically stands in a fixed relationship to the economic and political circumstances of the time. Moreover, one will not be able to claim, without providing detailed proof in each case, that law in action is a conspiracy of the haves against the have-nots. Even wide-sweeping legal reforms of supreme rulers who are out to change the nature of society cannot, in their individual rules of private law, be thought, without investigation in each particular, to embody precise and planned social, economic, or political messages. In truth, if we wish to understand a judicial decision, statute, or legal rule in any given society, we must consider not only the immediate social circumstances in which it arose but also the whole legal cultural background of the makers of the decision, statute, or rule. Unfortunately, if we then want to know precisely why the decision, statute, or rule is as it is, however original or revolutionary it may seem, we must often extend our gaze backward over centuries and into other countries. Only then are we in a position to determine precisely what message was intended to be conveyed.

But, to look on the brighter side, insights, flowing from the arguments, render explicable some puzzling phenomena in law. In this chapter, I seek first to explain two such phenomena that, puzzling though they otherwise are, now scarcely require explanation. Thereafter, in the final part of the chapter, I wish to apply the results of this and the preceding chapters to supply some plausible answers to perennial questions, in fact to explain in broad outline the pattern of development of English common law.

The first phenomenon that might have seemed puzzling but that, in light of the arguments of this book, may scarcely require explanation is the enormous role of the jurists—private individuals who were subject to almost no control—in the development of Roman private law. It is traditional to declare both that "praise of the excellence of Roman Law is always of Roman private law" and that "the private law was worked out and elaborated by first the pontiffs, a priestly college, and then the lay jurists in the most minute detail; . . . legislation played a very minor role in the development of Roman private law."[1] How can a state or government, so dynamic, so famous for the quality of its private law, so different in its nature at different epochs of its history, have left so much of its lawmaking in the hands of private individuals who held no official appointment?[2] The answer is first that the contribution of the jurists was precisely to private law, and second that states are often, as we have seen, uninterested in the precise content of much of law. Provided that someone takes care—to some extent—of the making of private law, and that the state can intervene when it wants to, the national authorities may allow much of the development of private law to take care of itself.

That is the first phenomenon that scarcely needs explaining. But the matter should not be left there. We have already seen in Chapter 2 how few statutes were passed in the later Roman Republic on private law. Certainly we should see the important reforms by the edicts of the higher elected officials, especially those of the praetors who had control of the law courts, as official intervention in the development of the law. But the edicts affecting law cannot be understood unless we emphasize again the role of the jurists. Thus, for instance, the praetor introduced into law the contract of sale by setting out model forms of action showing that he would grant remedies on a sale. But the edict does not lay down what constitutes a sale, the formalities for its formation, the essential requirements for the contract, the obligations of the parties, the interpretation of standard clauses, and so on. That is all left to the jurists. Again, to take another example, the edict *de peculio et de in rem verso* declared that an action lay against the *paterfamilias*, the Roman head of a family, regarding contracts made by his dependents up to the amount of their *peculium* (a fund a son or slave was allowed to use as his own, though it belonged to the *paterfamilias*) and the extent he benefited. But what was *peculium*, how it was created, how its extent was measured, what the son or slave could do with it, were all issues settled by the jurists. The praetorian Edict cannot be understood except in the light of the enormous power left to the jurists to build up the law.[3] But then, as we also saw in Chapter 2, the Byzantine Emperor Justinian, when he came to codify Roman law in the sixth century, had no intention of incorporating any precise political, social, or economic messages in the texts in the *Digest* that he extracted from the jurists.

But events were to take a turn that may appear even more astonishing. From the eleventh century onward until the era of codification, there was in Western continental Europe as a whole the great development known as the Reception of Roman law. This borrowing of Roman law was massive, as is generally agreed. Of course, the borrowing was not complete and was selective. But when that has been said, it should be stressed that in general the Reception was either, in effect, of the *Corpus Juris* as a whole (with exceptions where there was a contrary local statute of custom) or as it was glossed or as understood by Bartolus. It is only on this basis that we can have such works as Philibert Bugnyon's *Traicté des loix abrogées et inusitées en toutes les Cours du royaume de France* (first published in 1563, several times republished, with one edition as late as 1802), or the better-known Simon van Groenewegen, *Tractatus de legibus abrogatis et inusitatis in Hollandia vicinisque regioribus* (published in 1649; English translation for use in South Africa began to be published in 1974). It was thought to be useful in Holland and even in France, where the Reception was less complete, to have works detailing the rules of the *Corpus Juris* that were not received or used.

It is also only on this basis that we can explain the rule which came to be accepted in Germany: "Quidquid non agnoscit glossa non agnoscit curia," or whatever in the *Corpus Juris* was not glossed by the old Italian jurists was not recognized in the German courts. And it is on this basis too that we see the force of the *Ordenaçoes Filipinas* for Portugal in 1603 (which were already mentioned in Chapter 2) that Roman law together with the gloss of Accursius and the opinions of Bartolus were subsidiary law. But this wholescale Reception of Roman law as authoritative (as subsidiary law, in the absence of contrary custom or statute) means that there was a general lack of interest on the part of the state in any particular message in Roman private law. But again it must be emphasized that the Reception can only be massive if in general the law was not otherwise developing much by statute, which was the case.

But a further dimension must be added. Reception as a whole within a given territory can occur only by statute or custom. If the Reception is by statute, which is infrequently the case, then the ruler or legislature accepting Roman law as a whole or as glossed as subsidiary law clearly has no precise interest in the political, social, or economic messages of the individual rules. Nor should it be argued against this point that rulers had a special interest in receiving Roman law because Roman law was autocratic: what was received was only Roman private law.[4] If the Reception was by custom, as was ordinarily the case, as in Holland[5] and Scotland,[6] then the development of the law was, as in Rome of the later Republic and High Empire, very much in the hands of private jurists, though primarily university professors, since it was they whose opinion was accepted by the judges as giving the correct interpretation of the law. Incidentally, even when the Reception is by statute, it is still private jurists whose interpretation, accepted by judges, prevails. And, indeed, as was seen again in Chapter 2, when rulers pressed for codification from the eighteenth century onward, as in Bavaria and Prussia, what often was wanted was a reform of the sources of law, not its substance.

We have moved a considerable distance from the first phenomenon that I wished to examine in this chapter, which, I maintained, though apparently astonishing at first sight, scarcely required explanation. But it appears that not only in the formative period of Roman law was the main line of development of private law in the hands of individuals with no state appointment or responsibilities, but also that private jurists exercised the primary influence on continental legal development until at least the later eighteenth century. This is true even when the jurists rejected Roman law solutions.

I would not want to be misunderstood as denying that law is power, that a state can have vital interests in controlling courts or in particular rules. The point is that to a very great extent states can be indifferent to the substance of private law and leave its growth very much to individuals who do not hold the reins of government. Law certainly is politics in the sense that it is politics that decides who can make law and what the formulation of law is to be. But it is a fundamental error to conclude from that that law is a reflection of the political system.

The second phenomenon to be discussed concerns communication of the law. At the least, law and legal systems operate to promote order within a society by providing an institutionalized process for regulating disputes. At the most, they exist to direct the thought and behavior of individuals along channels approved by political superiors. In either case, one might expect that communication of both the rules and their purpose to the parties affected would be central to the notion of law. It turns out, however, that communication in law is much less prized.

The Western world has made use of four sources of law (in the sense of bases of legitimacy that courts habitually regard as determinative for their decisions): custom, judicial precedent, juristic opinion, and statute (including codes). Each source has different implications for communication.

The traditional theory of custom is that habitual behavior comes to have legal force when people observe it in the belief that it is already binding as law. In practice, a supposed custom becomes law when court decisions, based on it, become accepted as a statement of customary law. In fact, there may have been no preceding custom, people doing different things, or if there was, it may not have been widely known. Customary law usually is found primarily in small societies with no powerful central administration, and it is a typical

137

feature of customary legal systems that either the law is not known or there are many gaps in it. But a judge, faced with an issue, must decide the case before him, whether or not customary behavior provides an answer. The judge frequently borrows, as if it were the custom, a rule from an admired system or follows the opinion of a writer who is not authoritative and who frequently has made up a rule or borrowed one from elsewhere. Where custom reigns, law is not well known. When an authoritative account of custom is produced, it becomes law, but as statute. Custom is not a powerful source of law in the developed world today, but has been in continental Europe especially during the Middle Ages, and still is in parts of Africa and elsewhere.[7]

Judicial precedent as a form of lawmaking is not a satisfactory way of communicating knowledge of law and its aims. The law is buried in numerous cases contained in multiple volumes; and usually several cases must be studied to extract even the beginnings of a rule. Even when textbooks report judge-made law, they leave the impression that the cases must still be read. Law becomes very remote from the very people who are expected to follow the law. Besides, law created in this way cannot be systematic. But judge-made law is a poor communicator not just because it is difficult to find but also because it waits on events and decides what was the right thing to have done in the past according to the law, which then was unknown and unknowable. It is a feature of most systems in which judicial precedent is accorded lawmaking force—though much less of the American system—that judicial decisions are not policy oriented. Judicial precedent is a powerful source of law in the common law countries and is coming to be more highly regarded in civil law countries.

Juristic opinion has been a powerful source of law in ancient Rome, in the development of the learned law in medieval and later Europe, and still today in civil law countries and to a lesser, though still marked, extent in the United States. For communication, juristic opinion has the advantages that it can be forward looking, can set out an issue or a whole area of law systematically and clearly, and can formulate reasons for the adoption of rules. But it suffers from the defect that it is not law, and hence cannot be known to be the law until its authority is accepted by either a court or a legisla-

ture. Most systems that treat juristic opinion as important for finding the law fail to set up a system for deciding which jurists or
which opinions are to be given precedence when jurists disagree, as
is frequently the case. This was true, for instance, for ancient Rome
during most of the time when juristic opinion shaped legal change,
for most of the states of Western Europe during the centuries of the
Reception of Roman law before codification, and for present-day
Germany. Again, a juristic opinion often may come to shape the law
a considerable time after it was expressed. Thus, insofar as it is a
source of law, juristic opinion cannot be given high marks for communicating the law.

Legislation, at least in theory, can be the most powerful form of
lawmaking. It also has the greatest power to shape legal thought,
direct human behavior, and censor knowledge. Only legislation can
break sharply with preceding law and make a new beginning. A good
modern example, already mentioned in a different context, is the
adoption in 1925 of the Swiss civil code (with only minor modifi-
cations) by Atatürk, and the subsequent acceptance of commercial
law from similar European sources. Atatürk aimed at secularizing,
modernizing, and westernizing Turkey, and law was one of his tools.
Although these aims were not achieved at one stroke, nonetheless
the new law was successfully adopted. Moreover, not only can statute law seek to change human behavior, but the legislators can
make their purpose clear and set out their ends in a preamble—a
device apparently invented by Plato and favored by Jeremy Bentham,
though opposed by Frederick the Great and Lord Macaulay. Legislation, in addition, can be systematic concerning a single branch of
law or, as in modern codifications, can cover whole fields of law.

Thus, law, as communication, as an institutionalized way to regulate and direct human behavior, is best served by legislation. But
some features of legislation, which are typical according to the lesson of history and as noted in Chapter 2, should again be mentioned.
First, before modern times legislation usually was relatively rare.
Second, although legislation may break with the past, it does so only
at the time when it is promulgated. It is a feature of legislation, especially marked perhaps in codification, that once it is in place it
tends to remain unaltered, possibly for centuries. The courts may
reinterpret it away from its original purpose, but then the resulting

law is as difficult to find and know as any other judge-made law. Third, very little statute law and very few codes are original in the sense that they are made fresh for the territory in which they operate, without a great dependence on law from elsewhere. Atatürk's reforms are typical: it is easier to borrow than to create even if the law does not precisely dovetail the aims of the society. Whatever Atatürk may have desired, and whatever he may have achieved, few modern civilized societies were more different in geography, economy, politics, and religion than Switzerland at the turn of the century and Turkey in the 1920s. Yet the law of the one was taken over by legislation for the law of the other.[8] Fourth, even "original" legislation usually has hidden roots in the often distant past, roots that are not present in the consciousness of the legislator and that affect the attempt to direct behavior. Fifth, apart from topics of consuming passion to the legislators, legislators are generally not interested in law reform, especially in the field of private law. Change through legislation may be a long time coming.

Attention must also be called to a factor that appears at times in all forms of lawmaking and that demonstrates some lack of interest, to say the least, in communicating the contents of law to those affected by—namely, the redaction of law in a language inaccessible to many of those affected by it. For legislation, the instance *par excellence* must be Justinian's *Digest* and *Code*. At the time of their promulgation, and for centuries before, the center of empire was not the Roman West but the Greek East, and Latin was no longer the language of the bulk of the population, and was not even understood by the majority of those who might have problems of private law. But virtually all of the *Digest* is in Latin, as is by far the greater part of the *Code*. But Justinian at no time had plans to prepare a Greek version of these works.[9]

Other similar, powerful examples can be drawn from the Germanic so-called barbarian codes from the fifth century onward, such as the *Edictum Theoderici,* the *Codex Euricianus,* and *Liber iudiciorum* (or *Visigothic Code*) for the Visigoths, the *Lex Burgundionum* for the Burgundians, the *Lex Baiuwariorum* for the Bavarians, the *Lex Ribuaria* for the Riparian Franks, the *Lex Alamannorum* for the Allemani, and so on.[10] The French *code civil* was adopted in French as the law of the Dominican Republic in 1845 and was not translated into Spanish until 1884. For the use of a foreign language in a system when judicial precedent was important, we may refer to the use of French in English courts after the Conquest. At first this may have been reasonable, but it soon ceased to be so. Pollock and Maitland observe that in 1362 a statute that was itself in French "declared that as the French tongue was but little understood, all pleas should be 'pleaded, shown, defended, answered, debated and judged' in the English tongue. But this came too late."[11] For some time thereafter, even the law reports appeared only in French. For redactions of customary law, one might select as illustrations the *Coutume de Toulouse,* which was inscribed in Latin in the *livre blanc* kept in the Town Hall and was only fully translated into French at the end of the eighteenth century by Soulatges expressly to make it accessible to lawyers and others.[12] Or, to choose from only one part of medieval Spain, Extremadura, the fueros of Calatayud (1131), Daroca (1142), Teruel (1177), and Cuenca (1188 or rather later), again, all were in Latin. Yet redactors of customary law habitually give as a reason for writing down the customs the fact that they are easily forgotten. But how does it help to follow the custom if it is written in a language one does not understand?

The conclusion seems unavoidable even if surprising. In general, over much of the area of law, lawmakers are little concerned either to communicate the law and their message in it or even to have a particular message in it. For the latter point, the frequency and extent of legal borrowings are decisive. For the former, one might choose the illuminating example of criminal law in nineteenth-century England: if one wants an example of law used to communicate ideals of behavior and to influence conduct, then the desire to restrain behavior regarded as wrongful should have a special place. In 1833, criminal law commissioners were appointed in England with the initial task of showing the need to put statutory and common law principles in one code; then they had to prepare a restatement of the existing law in the code. Despite much previous legislation, a great deal of the law was judicial precedent and hard to find. Five reports were produced between 1839 and 1845, and a revised commission then produced another five reports between 1845 and 1849. Judges at that stage objected to the notion of a code as being too rigid a framework for the law. Members of Parliament, who also sat as jurors or as justices of the peace, also were unenthusiastic about reform. The final result was nothing more than a statute, 24 & 25 Victoria, Cs 94-100, consolidating the law that was already in statute.

All this was set against the background of a penal code for British India drafted by Lord Macaulay and successfully promulgated. Sir James Fitzjames Stephen, who had experience with the Indian codes, produced in the 1870s his own draft of a criminal code that at one time looked as though it would be successful before Parliament but was again defeated by the opposition of the judges. It did not pass in England but was a success in some colonies. Since then, there has been some, little and slow, progress.[13] Scholars may disagree as to the motivation of the reluctant lawmakers, whether as judges or legislators, but for us here the lesson is simply that they showed no great desire to communicate knowledge of what the law was or even to produce a precise message in the law. This lack of interest in communication on the part of lawmakers is typical.

Nor should one rush to conclude that present-day legislators are more eager to communicate knowledge of the law to their constituents. The example of England is instructive. The difficulties in finding out the law from English statutes has been a common refrain among those concerned with lawmaking, at the highest level, since at least the middle of the sixteenth century.[14] The difficulties are no less obvious today, and authoritative criticism is no less vociferous. To avoid the appearance of prejudice—and to avoid repeating what I have said elsewhere—I want here to make extensive use of one contemporary and authoritative author, Francis Bennion, who was formerly one of the Parliamentary Counsel and was chairman of the Statute Law Society from 1977–1979. He points out several deficiencies in communicating knowledge of the law. Among these are:

The British have never adopted for themselves the idea of a scientific statute book, by which I mean one kept up to date and arranged under Titles on a one-Act, one-subject basis. We have not changed from the system under which Acts are produced as required, with the subject matter of each being determined by the political and administrative convenience of the moment. Yet, strangely, a far superior system was imposed by Britain on the territories which formed part of the British empire. The independent countries of the Commonwealth, who inherited and developed this system, are the beneficiaries today.

As an example of the Colonial system, we may take the West African colony of the Gold Coast (now Ghana). British rule dated from 1827. The first collected edition of legislative texts was published in one volume in 1860. Thereafter, until British rule ended a century later, no fewer than nine collected and revised editions were promulgated. The practice was to enact in advance of each edition a Revised Edition of the Laws Ordinance. This authorized the editor (usually a retired judge or law officer) to combine texts into unified Titles, omit spent matter, and carry out other improvements. On being approved by the Governor, the new edition became "The sole and only proper Statute Book."[15]

What ought to be stressed, as Bennion makes us aware, is that the continuing weakness in communication is not the result of a failure either to see that communication of law may be beneficial or to know where a remedy lies. In the same context, he calls attention to the poor record of the British in producing satisfactory and timely consolidation acts.[16]

He also insists on the reluctance of the British drafting office to innovate:

The other example concerns the Interpretation Act 1978. A disgracefully long period had elapsed since the passing of the previous Act (the Interpretation Act 1889). Much complaint had been expressed over this quite unnecessary delay, which meant that many obsolete provisions continued to encumber the statute book. Other countries had developed this useful tool to a considerable degree. Even Northern Ireland, with exiguous resources, had been able to produce a very sophisticated model (the Interpretation Act [Northern Ireland] 1954 . . .). The adoption of these improvements by the United Kingdom Parliament was confidently looked forward to. The Renton Committee,[17] for example, after pointing out that without the 1954 Act subsequent Northern Ireland statutes would, upon a conservative estimate, be one-third larger than they are, called for a comprehensive revised Interpretation Act (Renton 1975, paras. 19.4–19.11, 19.31, 19.32). What happened? The 1978 Act, produced under the inspiration (if that is the word) of the Parliamentary Counsel Office, amounted to little more than straight consolidation of existing British enactments.[18]

Bennion lists and discusses four factors that block comprehension of statute law.[19] *Compression* of language is exceptionally highly prized but often baffles the reader. *Anonymity* is standard, in the sense that few signposts are provided for the reader. There are few headings and side notes and not enough cross-references, and typographical devices are not used to pick out key references. *Distortion* of structure and arrangement follows from techniques adopted to get the act through Parliament with as little debate as possible on critical features. The fourth factor he calls *Scatter*, which is the treatment of a topic in different places. But he then adds a fifth vice that he considers "a peculiarly British phenomenon"[20]—that the principal acts (as he calls them) are in practice amended indirectly, and not by altering the text of the principal act. This is a vice that has often been stressed before. It should be noticed, moreover, that this practice makes difficult not only the comprehension of the reader but also the comprehension of the legislator.[21]

It is as a counsel of despair that he suggests that "in default of the production of model clauses by an official keeper of the statute book, the job could be done by an unofficial body."[22] And he recommends as an example to the English legal profession the setting up in 1923 of the American Law Institute by judges and representatives of the American Bar Association.

To what has been said about the lack of interest on the part of the lawmakers to communicate law, however, three qualifications should be made.

First, a desire for communication seems a predominant motive in the minds of many who have sought successfully for a codification of the law. This is true, for example, of Moses, Hammurabi, Justinian, Frederick the Great, Napoleon, and Atatürk. It is also true of some who unsuccessfully sought codification, such as Julius Caesar and Jeremy Bentham. Dissatisfaction with the actual substance of the rules was usually a much lesser motivation. Usually the need to communicate the rules of law is made express by these reformers. Two features stand out: 1) Those who wish law communicated by codification usually stand outside the legal tradition—they are impatient with the tolerance of other lawmakers for obfuscation; and 2) They wish to communicate knowledge of law, not a particular social message in the law. Thus, even when Atatürk wished to westernize Turkey, the Swiss law was chosen as the model for the Turkish civil code, apparently for no greater reason than that the Turkish minister of justice had studied law in Switzerland. Frederick the Great expressly declared himself largely satisfied with the substance of the Roman law in force in Prussia. Napoleon's civil code is very much rooted in France's past. Justinian's *Digest* contains almost no texts that are not at least three hundred years old.

Second, in some countries, communication of some branches of law is taken so seriously that the countries may become almost best known even in the outside world for these legal attitudes: Ireland for its refusal to give legal recognition to divorce, its criminal sanctions against abortion and contraception; the Republic of South Africa for its laws against mixing the races. The legal rules will often be communicated in a simplified form through media such as radio or newspapers. The law in question is usually such as maintains social conditions and attitudes that are regarded by that state as vital to its interests and that distinguish it from other societies. The law is here used to communicate and preserve very particular social values. One cannot lay down general rules regarding the branches of law on which attention to communication will be focused. It is not the case that a special desire to communicate rules will always be seen in criminal law (as the example of nineteenth-century England shows) or in family law. Likewise, attention is not necessarily focused in capitalist societies on the clarity, or even the formation, of business law: the very late development in the nineteenth century of commercial law in England—to Max Weber's bewilderment—is sufficient proof of this.

Third, written constitutions typically are used to communicate the highest ideals or the propaganda values embraced by the leaders of a state. This is true for countries as diverse as the United States and the Soviet Union. In contrast to the rest of law, constitutions are usually not technical in their language, are widely disseminated in inexpensive or even free editions, and are often referred to rhetorically by politicians and others. They are treated as basic law, the knowledge of which is a duty for citizens. They are used to induce loyalty in the citizen to the state.

Thus, in conclusion, although law regulates human behavior and must be communicated in order to do so, society shows, in general, relatively little interest in making knowledge of the law accessible to those affected by it, or even in setting out clear aims in the law. This lack of interest in communication is best seen as indicating that the needs served in a particular society by law are above all the establishment of some kind of order, but not that some precise ordering of society is behind every law. To a considerable extent, law is an expression of the culture of the lawmaking elite, and in making law one lawmaker signals to another: judges write opinions for other judges or top practitioners, jurists write texts for other scholars, legislators legislate to impress other parliamentarians. Only in very particular circumstances do lawmakers attempt to set out a message in law for the populace at large or to set out the law clearly. Outside these particular circumstances, states seem interested largely in communicating only the most basic notions: "Thou shalt not steal"—but not the nature of the act and intention that constitutes theft; "Contracts are binding"—but not the definition of a contract or the rights and duties of a party under a contract.

Finally, it may be possible to capitalize on what has gone before to give a plausible explanation for the pattern of development of English common law. For convenience, we may start in 1066 with the invasion of England by William the Conqueror. To make the history of the common law in outline comprehensible, we need add only a minimum of historical information: the Norman Conquest was successful; it led to foreign domination with a ruling elite spread thin; and it led to military feudalism. All the rest follows.

To retain control over a subject people requires strong government, and to keep a sizable military force takes money. Provided the king's peace is kept and money is raised, a strong monarch need not be interested in the private lives or arrangements of the people. This lack of interest we have already seen. Indeed, why should he be interested in these matters? There are more exciting and enjoyable and pressing things to do. William decreed that all men were to have and hold the law of King Edward—that is, old English law—but with additions that William had made to it.[23] Pollock and Maitland declare:

> So far as we know, he expressly legislated about very few matters. He
> forbad the bishops and archdeacons to hold in the hundred courts

pleas touching ecclesiastical discipline; such pleas were for the future to be judged according to the canons and not according to the law of the hundred; the lay power was to aid the justice of the church; but without his leave, no canons were to be enacted and none of his barons or ministers excommunicated. He declared that his peace comprehended all men both English and Normans. He required from every free man an oath of fealty. He established a special protection for the lives of the Frenchmen; if the slayer of a Frenchman was not produced, a heavy fine fell on the hundred in which he was slain. He declared that this special protection did not extend to those Frenchmen who had settled in England during the Confessor's reign. He defined the procedural rules which were to prevail if a Frenchman accused an Englishman, or an Englishman a Frenchman. He decreed that the county and hundred courts should meet as of old. He decreed that every free man should have pledges bound to produce him in court. He forbad that cattle should be sold except in the towns and before three witnesses. He forbad that any man should be sold out of the country. He substituted mutilation for capital punishment. This may not be an exhaustive list of the laws that he published, nor can we be certain that in any case his very words have come down to us; but we have good reason to believe that in the way of express legislation he did these things and did little more.[24]

Not one of these enactments can be thought to deal with private law, except possibly that concerning the sale of cattle. But we can be sure that the purpose of this, as with earlier Anglo-Saxon laws on the subject,[25] was to protect the buyer from subsequent charges of cattle theft. It was no great concession for William to let the English keep their law. His behavior is paralleled by other conquerors. More to the point, those who can legislate for their own people often are little concerned with the private lives and arrangements of their people. The instance already addressed in Chapter 2 of the minor use made of legislation for private law in the Roman Republic is relevant. Likewise, we need not attribute the sparseness of private law legislation in medieval Spain or Germany to the weakness of the monarchy and an inability to change the law: rulers legislated often enough to grant charters and privileges.[26] Where the interests of the English king and his immediate followers were not directly involved he need not concern himself with the private lives of his subjects by legislating for their benefit or by establishing courts to settle their disputes.

Already, before the Conquest, in Anglo-Saxon times the ordinary courts were the county court, which met twice a year, and the hundred court, which met every four weeks.[27] The king did not do justice in the ordinary way but exercised a special jurisdiction that was not to be used unless someone failed to get his cause heard in his hundred.[28] Whether there already existed, as after the Conquest, numerous courts of lords is not clear.[29] The Normans took over the existing public jurisdiction, but the sheriff, in charge of the county court, came to be regarded as a servant of the king, to be kept in his place. "From presiding over what was, for all ordinary purposes, the most important kind of court in the land, he slowly became the executive addressee of commands from higher central bodies."[30] The hundred court, however, often came to be in private hands. It is estimated that by the accession of Edward I, more than half of the hundred were in private hands, though the lord might exercise considerable control or be entitled only to a share in the profits of justice.[31]

The county courts of the hundred were as much instruments of government as courts in the modern sense, and these courts were governed by the king. Government at the upper level was largely a matter of financial accounting for what became due to the king from lower lords.[32] The system developed of journeys by the king's commissioners, of justices in eyres, to check on the accounts given by the counties; and likewise, within each county, the sheriff checked on the hundreds. This system of traveling justice was necessary, not just to raise the money needed for royal expenditure but also to control the power of great local magnates. The business of the eyre came to be of two kinds. The more important involved the pleas of the crown, in which the king could have a direct financial interest; the other involved common pleas, disputes between ordinary litigants. This second kind was at first exceptional, and it always required the special authorization of a writ.[33]

Royal central courts also begin to emerge, with their origins again in itinerant government. The king himself frequently had to be on the move about his kingdom, and from his council that traveled with him there gradually developed the king's bench, which, however (as Milsom observes), could not be a regular channel for royal justice as long as it was in constant movement.[34] But it, too, heard two kinds of cases, those in which the king had a direct interest and common pleas. The Magna Carta, c.17. was to decree that hearings of common pleas were not to follow the person of the king but were to be held in a certain place, and this was to lead to the establishment of a Court of Common Pleas. This came to have exclusive jurisdiction, because common pleas could not be heard before the Court of the King's Bench, which was held wherever the king was in England.

This evolution was absolutely "natural" and to be expected in the circumstances. Little interest would be shown in the development of ordinary private law, local public courts (county and hundred) would remain in place but would, of necessity if the usurpers were to reign, be brought under royal control primarily for purposes of revenue and for keeping the king's peace—but extraordinarily also for ordinary suits between citizens. The mechanisms for controlling the local courts would need to be mobile and free from too much pressure from powerful local magnates, but would give rise to centralized state institutions with the right to hear lawsuits. These centralized state institutions, in their guise as royal courts, would have different jurisdictions from the local courts.

But if this evolution is "natural," we can deduce from it two immediate consequences that are, overall, inevitable. First, some organizational system would have to be devised to determine which court had jurisdiction in a particular case. This was in fact to be the system of writs. Thus, very great emphasis would be placed on the issue of jurisdiction. Of central importance to the parties in any dispute would be how it could be brought before some particular court. Substantive law, when it did develop, would develop from the basis of a jurisdictional right, rather than from a theoretical understanding of the nature of a legal institution, such as a sale or hire. Again, as we know from other systems and other legal issues, the organizational system determining jurisdiction would ossify.

Second, in order to fix jurisdiction, abundant use would have to be made of legal fictions, especially during and after the ossification of the organizational system determining jurisdiction. These fictions would be of two overlapping types: first, to establish a right of action for a particular situation where no right of action existed, and second, to bring a dispute before a particular court. Whichever type of fiction is involved, one result is to render obscure any theoretical

149

understanding of a legal institution. Side by side with fictions will develop dodges and devices of all kinds.

Something more must be said about each of these two consequences, beginning with writs, the organizational system developed to found jurisdiction. Naturally enough, we find that no writ was originally needed, only a simple complaint, to found jurisdiction in the county court.[35] But writs came to be needed for matters that could be conveniently treated there but that were not within its usual authority:

> This probably came to happen most often when the royal courts themselves began to hear private disputes as a regular thing. Lines of demarcation emerged between local and royal jurisdictions, depending upon the amount at stake or upon some royal interest; and if a plaintiff preferred to sue in the court on a matter lying on the royal side of the boundary, the sheriff could not act without the authority of a viscontiel writ.[36]

More important for late development, says Milsom, were writs in the king's courts, and he claims that many consequences flowed from the need for a writ being the accidental result of the Court of Common Pleas' earliest business being outside of the ordinary course of things:

> And it explains a great deal of inflexibility in the scope of the law, the kinds of matters with which it could deal at all. However much royal and central justice had started as something exceptional, as it became more and more the regular thing, the court slowly established a monopoly. It was not merely the body to which private disputes could conveniently be sent; they could not normally be sent to any other central court, for example, the king's bench. Partly this was the familiar hardening of practice into right, but partly it was a matter of "due process." When the Great Charter required common pleas to be held in some fixed place, it was perhaps mainly concerned with the need of the plaintiff to have access to justice. But there was also the defendant to consider. Litigation in a travelling court could be intolerable; and even when the king's bench came increasingly to rest, great men and great corporations, who retained standing attorneys in the common pleas, could argue that they should not be forced elsewhere. The paradoxical result was that the regular court to which ordinary disputes had to go was a court which could not act without special authority in each case, namely a writ from the chancery.[37]

And he adds:

> This jurisdictional accident was to be of growing consequence. In the middle ages it hampered the expansion of the common law by restricting the kinds of claims that could be brought before the court. If ordinary private disputes had continued to come before a jurisdiction like that of the eyre, to which plaintiffs had direct access, the common law could have reacted directly to changing needs; and in particular it could have continued to admit kinds of claims familiar in local courts but at first regarded as inappropriate for royal judges. But plaintiffs could not get to the court without a chancery writ, and the formulae of the writs, most of which were highly practical responses to the needs of thirteenth century litigants, became an authoritative canon which could not easily be altered or added to. Important areas, some new but many older than the king's courts themselves, were in this way cut off from legal regulation; and they could later be reached only by devious ingenuity in the common law courts, or by resorting to the chancellor's equitable jurisdiction to which once more the litigant could directly complain.
>
> All this was no more than the constriction of red tape. But so complete did it become that in the eighteenth century it engendered a purely formalistic view of the law and of its development which has lasted until our own day.

The question of jurisdiction and the relevant writ has a decisive impact on legal development. For each situation there is either one writ or no writ. There cannot be more than one appropriate writ. The royal courts will remain selective in the matters over which they exercise jurisdiction. Hence they will not be concerned with serfs or unfree land. Their interest in wrongs will largely be restricted to those which breach the king's peace, and much of contract law will be beyond their ambit.

Legal expertise will stress jurisdictional issues: which court is to hear a dispute, the scope of a writ. Discussion will focus on the boundaries of jurisdiction, not on the central core of an institution. Once a case comes before a royal court, discussion will be on the nature of the remedy, not on rules or principles. Technicalities, enforced by precedent, will breed frustration: at types of cases that cannot be heard when closely similar ones can, at arbitrary distinctions to found jurisdiction, at minute differences of fact that, when a case is heard, will bar relief in one but not in another, though the societal interest is the same. Dodges and devices of all kinds, legal fictions of all sorts, will emerge.

> The life of the common law has been in the abuse of its elementary ideas. If the rules of property give now what seems an unjust answer, try obligation; and equity has proved that from the materials of obligation you can counterfeit the phenomena of property. If the rules of contract give what now seems an unjust answer, try tort,

says Milsom.[38]

Exceptions upon exceptions upon exceptions will be commonplace. The great case will attract attention—where a court by subtle or sophisticated reasoning finds a new way out of the morass. And all honor to the judges. But in such a setting, the nature of a legal institution, legal rules and principles can be neither easily established nor easily set out. The law can be explained but not "rationally" analyzed. It will not even be an attractive task to write a book on a body of law. Any book that is written will show the concerns of practitioners.

Legal issues, when the royal courts do not accept jurisdiction, will fail to give rise to established law. There is no other recognized national authority. Entire areas of law, such as contract, will remain underdeveloped.

Fictions arise to alleviate particular hardships or for other jurisdictional reasons. Thus, since for wrongs to come before the king's court, the wrong had to be against the king's peace *vi et armis*, setting up an artificial barrier, it came in time to be standard practice to allege that a wrong was committed *vi et armis* when it was not. Even some breaches of contract will be handled in this way.[39] Again, to found jurisdiction in the king's bench, which, once it ceased to be mobile, always sat in Middlesex, the fictitious complaint of a trespass in Middlesex will be made.[40] Whatever advantages would accrue both in particular cases and in general, a consequence of fictions is to skew the law.

This concentration on jurisdiction, devices, fictions, and technicalities will isolate the law. Since, apart even from technical issues of jurisdiction, particular circumstances of fact in a lawsuit will condition judicial response, which then has an impact on subsequent judicial decisions on different facts, English common law will look very different from other systems and would even look very different from a system that developed on a similar basis. Foreign systems of law, including Roman law, can have relatively little impact. They may influence particular decisions, but whole institutions, such as the notion of possession or the contract of partnership, cannot be inserted. The common law becomes impenetrable except to those already expert in it. Even the English, living in the system but not as lawyers, cannot understand it and hence have difficulty in even suggesting reform. Practicing lawyers, above all the judges who control the working of the system, come to regard the law as their holy mystery and are proud of its separateness. They strongly resent and deprecate legislation. It cannot surprise us that the language of the law remained Anglo-French centuries after it became incomprehensible to others.[41]

This simple division of jurisdiction between the royal courts and other courts, with the former restricting their intervention only to certain kinds of issues, is enough to explain the main features of English common law as it developed.

It determined the extreme interest in jurisdictional issues, in the technicalities of getting the issue to court, and in points of pleading.

It cut across what otherwise could have been seen as a unitary branch of the law, such as tort or contract. Thus, such a branch of the law could not be seen as a whole: what mattered was what remedy was available, and in what court.

It thus insured that for long the common law could scarcely be regarded as a fit subject for intellectual analysis and rational explanation. The field was thus left more or less completely in the hands of practitioners who concentrated on matters before them.

It blocked the Reception of Roman law as a system based on separate institutions of private law, rules, and principles.[42]

It hindered the development of entire areas of law, such as contract law. People could make contracts, even litigate them, but there was no recourse to the royal courts, which had national authority.

Finally, it was a handicap to the writing of books in entire areas of law that had scarcely developed, thus further handicapping development.

This explanation of the course of development of English common law and of its characteristics proceeds easily from a few basic historical facts, once it is accepted that kings and other legislators need have no interest in the law provided the public peace is kept (and revenues roll in), that much of lawmaking can therefore be safely entrusted to persons not in the higher levels of government, and that the ruling elite need not worry too much if the substance of the law is not easily communicable to those affected by it.

Chapters 1 and 3 of this book were originally conceived of as dealing with particular failures of the legal imagination as significant examples of a much wider phenomenon. But writing Chapter 2 to link these, and Chapter 4 to show law developing despite failures, convinced me that something more was involved. It is not just, as I have argued elsewhere, that the available means of making law are frequently inadequate to their task and that this is not remedied even when the inadequacy is clearly known to those able to do something about it.[43] From one angle, that of efficiently running and controlling the state, the supreme rulers need have little concern with most of the substance of private law,[44] or even of how the law operates in practice. It is enough that they can control law when they want. From this viewpoint, there is no failure of the legal imagination when rulers either fail to introduce much-needed legislation at all or fail to insert in it the most appropriate political message. From another angle, of course, from the perspective of the well-being of their subjects (who in a sense are the consumers of the product, law), there is a failure of the legal imagination. The ruling elite often does not regard lawmaking as a task entrusted to it for the common good. Judges and jurists, in their turn, have their failures, too, treating law as their cultural preserve.[45]

NOTES TO CHAPTER 6

1. J. A. C. Thomas, *Textbook of Roman Law* (Amsterdam: North Holland, 1976), pp. 4f.

2. Elsewhere, I have dealt twice with the stages in the development of private law by the jurists, and this development need not be sketched again here: see Watson, *Sources of Law, Legal Change, and Ambiguity* (Philadelphia: University of Pennsyl-

vania Press, 1984), pp. 2ff., and review of B. Frier, *The Rise of the Roman Jurists* in *Michigan Law Review* 85 (1987):1071ff. The most recent writer on the *ius respondendi* is in basic agreement with the view expressed in *Sources of Law:* F. Wieacker, "Respondere ex auctoritate principis," in *Satura Roberto Feenstra,* ed. J. A. Ankum, J. E. Spruit, and F. B. J. Wubbe (Fribourg: éditions universitaires Fribourg, 1985), pp. 71ff.

3. See, e.g., Watson, review of Frier, *The Rise of the Roman Jurists.*

4. For those who believe that Roman law was sought by rulers because it was autocratic, an interesting problem is created by the example of France, where Roman law was more influential and rested on a different basis in the *pays de droit écrit* than in the *pays de droit coutumier.* For the German emperor, there could be ideological reasons for regarding the Empire as a continuation of the Roman Empire, but these do not extend to an explanation of why German law, fitted to German conditions, did not develop, but instead a private law gradually encroached.

5. See, e.g., Grotius, *Inleidinge tot de hollandsche rechtsgeleertheyd* (1631), 1.2.2.2; Groenewegen, *Tractatus, ad Inst. 1.6.3.*

6. Lord Stair, *Institutions of the Law of Scotland* (1681), 1.11; 1.15; G. Mackenzie, *Institutions of the Law of Scotland* (1684), 1.1.

7. See Watson, *Evolution,* pp. 43ff.

8. See A. Watson, "The Evolution of Law: Continued," *Law and History Review* 5 (1987): 537ff. at 550ff.

9. In this context, a suggested explanation that Justinian was conservative must be insufficient.

10. Again in this context, the failure to produce versions in the various Germanic languages cannot simply be shrugged off by saying that, in view of the predominance of Roman law, Latin was the obvious language for legal works.

11. Pollock and Maitland, *History,* 1, p. 85.

12. *Coutume de Toulouse* undated, but the latest reference is to 10 November 1769.

13. On this, see, e.g., W. R. Cornish in Coing, *Handbuch,* 3, pp. 2225ff.; F. Bennion, *Statute Law,* 2nd ed. (London: Longman, 1883), pp. 74f.

14. For some references, see Watson, *Sources of Law,* pp. 77ff.

15. *Statute Law* (London: Oyez Longman, 1982), p. 73.

16. Ibid., pp. 73ff.

17. This committee was set up by the British government in 1973 to achieve greater simplicity and clarity in statute law.

18. Ibid., pp. 24f.

19. Ibid., pp. 119ff.

20. Ibid., p. 131. But it is not in fact confined to Britain.

21. See, for an example, the discussion in A. Watson, "A House of Lords' Judgment, and Other Tales of the Absurd," *American Journal of Comparative Law* 33 (1985): pp. 673ff., especially from p. 683.

22. *Statute Law,* p. 29.

23. Laws of William (select chapters) c.7: see, e.g., F. Pollock and F. W. Maitland, *History,* 1, p. 88; J. H. Baker, *Introduction to English Legal History,* 2nd ed. (London:

Butterworths, 1979), p. 11. It is not my intention to challenge accepted notions of the course of development of English law. Hence to make my account acceptable I shall, as far as possible, rely on quotations from the most highly regarded authorities.

24. Pollock and Maitland, *History*, 1, p. 88.

25. Ibid., p. 59.

26. For the argument, see Watson, "Evolution of Law: Continued."

27. See Pollock and Maitland, *History*, 1, p. 42.

28. See Ibid., pp. 40f.

29. See Ibid., p. 43.

30. See Milsom, *Foundations*, p. 14.

31. Ibid., p. 15.

32. Ibid., p. 26.

33. Ibid., pp. 28f.

34. Ibid., pp. 31f.

35. See, e.g., Milsom, *Foundations*, p. 33.

36. See Milsom, *Foundations*, p. 33.

37. Ibid., pp. 35f.

38. Ibid., p. 6.

39. Ibid., pp. 286ff.

40. Ibid., pp. 62ff.

41. See Pollock and Maitland, *History*, 1, pp. 80ff.

42. In consequence, it also blocked the use of the *Libri feudorum*, which in Europe came to be attached to the *Corpus Juris Civilis*. This had considerable consequences: see Watson, "The Evolution of Law: Continued," pp. 562ff.

43. Watson, *Sources of Law*.

44. This must not be construed as failing to recognize that law is power or that law is politics.

45. See A. Watson, "Legal Change," especially from p. 1151.

INDEX

Acceptilatio, 42
Accursius, 46f.
actio de effusis, 7f., 27, 73
actio de pastu, 9, 17
actio de pauperie, 8f., 73
actio de positis, 8
actio in factum, 43, 72
actus, 90
adoption, 94f.
adstipulator, 42
aediles, 9
Alexander Severus, 48
Alfenus, 75
Alfonso X, 46
American Law Institute, 144
Antoninus Pius, 70
aquae ductus, 90
Aquinas, 110
Archagathus, 67
Argou, G., 25
artes liberales, 68f., 77ff.
Asclapon, 69
Atatürk, 48, 53f., 139f., 144f.
Augustus, 37
Austin, J., 107f., 121ff.

Barbeyrac, 24
Bartolus, 46f., 135

bastard, 56
Bavaria, 58, 136
Beccaria, 58
Bennion, F., 142ff.
Bentham, J., 56, 58f., 126, 139, 144
Berlier, 52
Bernard, A., 77
Bexon, 58
BGB, 20
Bigot-Préameneu, 24
Blackstone, W., 58, 121, 123
Brazil, 46f.
Brissaud, J., 2
Bugnyon, P., 135

Calatayud, 141
Cambacérès, 56f.
capitis deminutio, 95
cas fortuit, 23
Cato, 66f.
cause, 25f.
cause étrangère, 23
cautio, 10
census, 97
Chronological Table, 39f.
Cicero, 68, 77
Cocceji, S., 50
Code (Justinian), 48f., 67f., 140

Code (Russian), 54f.
Code civil (France), 3ff. 35, 41, 50f., 56ff., 79, 140
Code civil (Sardinia), 23
Codex Euricianus, 140
Codex Theodosianus, 70
Codice civile (Italy), 23
Codigo civil (Brazil), 47
Codigo civil (Dominican Republic), 23, 140
coemptio, 93, 96
comitia calata, 92
comitia centuriata, 40
Commodus, 70
Common Pleas, 148ff.
communication, 137ff.
community property, 51f., 56
Compton, E., 99
concilium plebis, 40
confarreatio, 93
Constantine, 70
Cornish, W. R., 39
Corpus Juris Civilis, 6, 50, 135
County Court, 148f.
Coutume de Paris, 51f.
Coutume de Toulouse, 141
Coutumes de Normandie, 2
Crossman, A., 99
Cuenca, 141
custom, 1, 35, 118, 124f., 135ff.

damnum infectum, 9f., 18f.
damnum iniuria datum, 13f., 71ff.
Daroca, 142
delict, 3ff.
Denning, Lord, 98ff.
Digest (Justinian), 26, 48f., 65, 69, 75, 135, 140, 145
Diósdi, G., 91
divorce, 56
Domat, J., 11ff., 21, 26
dowry, 51, 53
Dumont, 58

Edict, 9f., 39f., 42, 135
edict *de peculio*, 135
edictum generale, 41, 71
Edictum Theoderici, 140
Edward, king, 146

emancipatio, 94
English law, 39, 43ff., 47, 87, 98ff., 141ff., 145ff.
error in substantia, 24f.
Esen, B. N., 54

Familiae emptor, 92f.
family council, 56
Favard, 24
fictions, 149f., 152
fiducia, 91, 96
Fifty Decisions, 49
force majeure, 23
Frederick the Great, 48f., 139, 144f.
Fuero Juzgo, 46
Fuero Real, 46
furtum, 13

Gaius, 42, 73, 75f., 88f., 91f., 95
Germany, 50, 54, 136, 139, 147
Ghana, 143
gloss, 136
Greuille, B. de, 17ff.
Groenewegen, S. van, 135
Grotius, H., 114f.
Guarano, M., 13, 65
Gürpinar, N. Y., 54

Hadrian, 95
Hammurabi, 144
Hansard, 99f.
Hart, H., 107f.
Hearnshaw, F. J. C., 126f.
Henry VIII, 44f.
hire, 38
Holland, 135f.
Hundred Court, 145, 147

Imperitia, 65f., 79
iniuria, 13, 41, 71
Institutes (Justinian), 2, 48, 65, 75
international law, 118, 123ff.
Interpretation Act, 143
Ireland, 145
iter, 90
ius commune, 1f.

Julian, 73
Julius Caesar, 144

jurisdiction, 147ff.
juristic opinion, 35f., 87ff., 134ff., 138f.
justice in eyre, 148, 158
Justinian, 48f., 68, 73, 135, 140, 146

Kaser, M., 93
Kelsen, H., 108
King's Bench, 148ff., 152

Latino, C., 120
Law of Property Act, 45
legislation, 35ff., 87, 112ff., 139ff.
Lei da Boa Razão, 47
Lex Alammanorum, 140
lex Appuleia, 37
lex Aquilia, 6f., 13f., 17, 27, 37, 39, 41f.,
   47, 65ff.
lex Atilia, 38
lex Atinia, 38
Lex Baiuwariorum, 140
Lex Burgundionum, 140
lex Canuleia, 41
lex Cicereia, 38
lex Cincia, 38
lex Cornelia, 38
lex Cornelia de sicariis, 43, 79
lex Falcidia, 38
lex Furia, 37f.
lex Minicia, 38
lex Plaetoria, 38
Lex Ribuaria, 140
lex Scribonia, 38
lex Voconia, 38
libel, 47
Luca, G. de, 13

Macaulay, Lord, 141, 146f.
Mackenzie, G., 13
Magna Charta, 149
Maitland, F. W., 141, 146f.
Maleville, 52
mancipatio, 88ff.
mandate, 38
manumission, 96f.
marriage, 93
Mela, 76
membrum ruptum, 41, 71f.
Milsom, S. F. C., 22, 47, 98, 150ff.
Miot, 15

missio in possessionem, 10f.
Modestinus, 69
Montesquieu, 58, 65f., 79
Morison, W. L., 126
mortis causam praestare, 43
Moses, 144
mule driver, 76

Napoleon, 48, 50f., 58, 144f.
natural law, 109ff., 124
Nerva, 88
nexum, 94
Noodt, G., 66
Normandy, 51
Northern Ireland, 143
noxal surrender, 6f., 9, 18

obedience, 120ff., 126
occidere, 43
ombudsman, 99
Ordenações Filipinas, 41, 46f., 136
os fractum, 41, 71f.

Pandektenrecht, 54f., 97f.
Parker, R., 2
partnership, 38
Pasquier, E., 53
paterfamilias, 66f., 72, 93, 135
patria potestas, 6f.
pays de droit coutumier, 51f.
pays de droit écrit, 51f.
peculium, 135
Pennsylvania, 58
Plato, 109f., 139
politics, 137
Pollock, F., 141, 146f.
Portugal, 46f., 136
positive law, 107ff.
Pothier, R., 14, 16, 24ff.
precedent, 35, 87, 138f.
Proculians, 89
Proculus, 75, 88
Prosser on Torts, 20
Prussia, 136
Pufendorf, S., 114ff., 123ff., 126

quasi-delict, 3ff.

Rapina, 13
Reception, 2ff., 40, 87, 97f., 135ff., 153

Regnaud, 19
Renton Committee, 143
Roman law, 2ff., 37ff., 53, 65ff., 88ff., 134ff.
Rudden, B., 40
Russia, 54f., 58f.

Sabinians, 89
sale, 38
sanction, 108ff., 116f., 119ff.
Savatier, 76
Scarman, Lord, 100f.
Schlesinger, R. B., 2f.
Schwarz, A., 126
Scotland, 47, 136
Seneca, 69
servitudes, praedial, 90, 96
Servius, 68
Seven Years' War, 50
Siete Partidas, 46
Singer, P., 125
slander, 47
slave, 6, 14, 37, 43, 66ff., 74ff., 80, 96f.
Soulatges, 141
South Africa, 135, 145
sovereign, 108ff., 116, 119ff.
Soviet Union, 54
Spain, 46, 147
Statute of Uses, 41, 44f., 47

Stephen, J. F., 142
Strauss, G., 50
Suárez, F., 109ff., 115, 118, 124, 126f.
succession, 42, 55, 95

Tarrible, 17
Teffaine case, 15
Teruel, 141
Toullier, 15
traditio, 90
Türk Kanunu Medenisi, 54
tutelage, 95
Twelve Tables, 41f., 70f., 91ff.

Ulpian, 72f., 75f., 78
U.S.A., 58, 70, 138, 145
U.S.S.R., 145

Via, 90f.
vi et armis, 152
Viollet, P., 2
Visigothic Code, 41, 46, 140

Weber, M., 145
Wieacker, F., 50
William the Conqueror, 146f.
wills, 9f.
Windscheid, B., 55, 97
writs, 150ff.